HIG... ...AY
ST...

ASSESSMENT AND
EVALUATION
OF LITERACY LEARNING

LEANNA TRAILL

The author wishes to acknowledge the help of friends, teachers, and children from the New Zealand Ministry of Education and the following New Zealand elementary schools:

Mangere Bridge – Auckland

Mt. Eden Normal – Auckland

Deanwell – Hamilton

Written by Leanna Traill

Editorial Development by Carol Hosking
Patty Whitehouse, Pat Kenison,
Linda Rourke, Janine Scott

Photography by Southcoast Gumboots,
Richmond, VICT. Australia (cover); David Lowe;
Dianne Repp; and Mike Brosilow

Design by Design Plural, Inc., Chicago, IL

Published by Rigby, a division of
Reed Elsevier Inc., Crystal Lake, IL

Distributed in the United States of America by

RIGBY
P.O. Box 797
Crystal Lake, IL 60039-0797
800-822-8661

Printed in the United States of America

ISBN 0 435 05321 3

My cat goed up the tree and it got stuck.

HIGHLIGHT MY STRENGTHS

ASSESSMENT AND EVALUATION OF LITERACY LEARNING

LEANNA TRAILL

CONTENTS

Letter from Leanna

Tena koe. Ōku mihi mahana kia koe.
My warm greetings to you.

This book is really about valuing children and trusting every child as a learner. It presents a view of evaluation of literacy acquisition as a whole pervasive and persuasive process within educational practice, one that is rooted in value and worth, founded on sound knowledge and theory of natural learning, and responsive to the goal of literacy for all of today's children in tomorrow's world.

My first teaching position, 28 years ago in New Zealand, was with a class of—dare I say it?—"backward" children. These were children labeled as backward, based on the findings of an I.Q. test. They were not backward; they were different. They were affectionate, lively, and volatile children, who brought to school with them diverse experiences and interests beyond their years, unabashed curiosity, and a wealth of energy to be harnessed.

I intuitively believed that for children to develop as successful learners at school I had to first create environmental contexts and conditions for learning that showed each and every one of them that I cared deeply for who they were and valued their own unique knowledge and experiences.

Somewhere in my growing, and quite definitely in my teaching, I learned always to look at children through positive-tinted lenses. I learned that by focusing on the strengths, weaknesses do indeed disappear.

The philosophy and principles of evaluation throughout this book are based on a holistic view of teaching and learning and are aligned with those of Rigby's Literacy 2000.®

Literacy 2000 — the resource — trusts children

Literacy 2000 — the goal — trusts teachers

The assessment procedures and strategies for observing, recording, and interpreting learning behavior focus on highlighting strengths. They are by no means a finite list, but they are those I know to be tried and true, and most effective in improving teaching for learning.

To help you be most effective in bringing together the goal and the resource, Rigby Education has put together a comprehensive teacher development evaluation package.

It is my desire that this entire evaluation package will provide you with a holistic and cohesive framework for thinking about, planning, and implementing systems for assessment and evaluation in a natural learning environment.

Leanna Traill

The Rigby Evaluation Package consists of the following components:

- *Highlight My Strengths: Assessment and Evaluation of Literacy Learning* — Leanna Traill
- Two videos
    - *Video 1: Learning Running Records* — Leanna Traill
    - *Video 2: Using Running Records* — Leanna Traill
- Class sets of folders for individualized Cumulative Learning Profile records
- Record pads: Each of the ten records discussed in the book is reproduced as a pad
- Class sets of home reading carriers
- Class sets of bookmarks for individualized home reading
- Vinyl carrying case

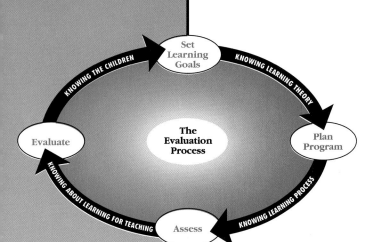

Introduction

The fundamental goal of teaching and learning in schools should be that every learner is guaranteed optimal instruction and opportunity to reach his or her educational potential. Assessment and evaluation practices are legitimate only to the extent that they serve this goal.

Children come into our care having already demonstrated extraordinary ability to make sense of the world around them, to construct their own meaning and knowledge, and to create their own realities.

In the process, they have shown an innate ability to think, to comprehend, to remember, to imagine, to create stories in their minds, to question, to talk, and to learn. They bring with them their own personal "knowing," their own dispositions, and a treasure of experiences, interests, strengths, and potential on which learning and teaching in school should be founded.

We must create educational environments that nurture and trust children as natural learners, that foster collaboration and the notion of community, while building on the uniqueness of individuality—educational envi-

> **Whaka paohotia ōku painga, kia ngaro ōku ngoikoretanga.***
> **"HIGHLIGHT MY STRENGTHS, AND MY WEAKNESSES WILL DISAPPEAR."**
> ***A Maori saying**

ronments that are responsive to the diverse interests and learning preferences of individuals and/or groups of children. Such contexts for learning enable children to grow tall and strong in all their emotional, physical, social, intellectual, and spiritual dimensions.

THE EVALUATION PROCESS

The terms *assessment* and *evaluation* as related to systems for educational accountability are frequently depicted as one and the same. This can create confusions and misunderstandings among teachers about the whole process and exact purposes of constructive evaluation.

Dictionary meanings show that the two words are generally synonymous, but that there is a subtle difference. The meanings that follow, selected from Webster's Ninth New Collegiate Dictionary, show this.

Assessment: critical appraisal for the purpose of understanding or interpreting, or as a guide to taking action.

Evaluation: the process of determining or fixing the value of.

For the purpose of this book, *assessment* is defined as the process of observing and accumulating objective evidence of an individual child's progress in learning. *Evaluation* is defined as the process of making judgments about the effectiveness of teaching for learning on the basis of credible, objective assessment. Evaluation in this context is both a component of the process and the process itself.

Within the evaluation process there are four clearly defined phases, each phase distinct from the others, yet interdependent one with the others; the quality of one will affect the quality of the others.

- *Set learning goals*—Specify learning goals based on knowledge of the children.

- *Plan program*—Plan specific learning experiences that will enable learners to progress toward the specific goals.

- *Assess*—Observe and collect information in a variety of ways and in a variety of contexts that will show a learner's progress toward the learning goals.

- *Evaluate*—Make judgments about the effectiveness of teaching for learning on the basis of this assessment information. This in turn guides and shapes the formation of new instructional goals.

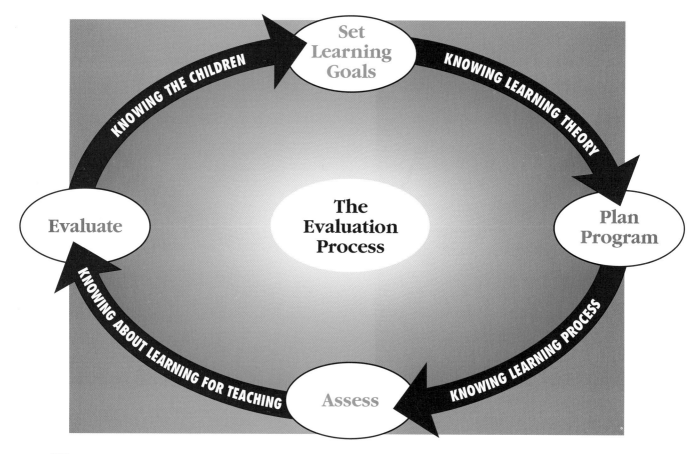

ASSESSMENT

Assessment is the process of observing and accumulating objective evidence of an individual child's progress in learning.

Purposes:

- to know the child

- to identify a child's strengths

- to observe a child's interactions with others

- to observe personal preferences and choices in self-selected activity

- to observe and record the behavior of learning, as well as the learned behavior

- to provide feedback and support for the learner

- to identify need for early intervention for children experiencing consistent difficulty

- to provide a professional, objective, honest profile of a child's progress in learning

Beliefs:

- Ultimate respect for the uniqueness and wholeness of each child must be at the center of all assessment procedures.

- It is ongoing, objective, integrated, reflective, descriptive, and honest.

- Process and product are valued.

- It is a collaborative, interactive process, encouraging the child to develop the habit of critical reflection and self-evaluation.

- Information is gathered and recorded in a variety of contexts.

- Perceptive analysis of learning behaviors forms the basis for instructional decisions.

- The teacher is the observer, collaborator, and instructional decision maker in the classroom.

EVALUATION

Evaluation means making judgments about the effectiveness of teaching for learning on the basis of credible objective assessment.

Purposes:

- to guarantee optimal educational instruction for all children

- to improve environmental contexts for learning and teaching

- to improve the selection and utilization of resources and materials

- to determine appropriate teaching approaches and strategies

- to set goals for teacher support and professional development

- to shape school decision making about school policy, management, organization, curriculum, and community inclusion

- to judge the effectiveness of assessment procedures in obtaining the most instructionally useful information about learning and teaching

Beliefs:

- Evaluation must be founded on *value* and *worth*.

- The key focus is on improving teaching and learning.

- It is an ongoing, integral, pervasive, and persuasive component of educational practice.

- It must be cognizant of individual and group preferred learning styles, cultural differences, expectations, attitudes, values, and knowledge.

- It is a collaborative, interactive, descriptive process involving the learner, peers, parents/caregivers, administrators, and teacher.

CUMULATIVE LEARNING PROFILE • CLP

A Cumulative Learning Profile is an organized synthesis of records that provides an authentic professional account of a learner's progress and development in learning over a period of time.

Purposes:

- to provide a portfolio of records that show the achievement and progress in learning by an individual child over time

- to present authentic data on which to base reflective discussion about processes of learning and learned behavior with the learner, parents/caregivers, colleagues, principals, and administrators

- to provide a receiving teacher (or school) with credible background

Watching children and gathering information in a variety of ways from within a variety of contexts helps build an authentic profile of a child's attitudes, strengths, and needs in learning development.

information about a learner's attitudes, strengths, and starting points for further development

- to enable a learner to evaluate his/her own progress in learning

- to enable a teacher to evaluate his/her own effectiveness in teaching

Beliefs:

- A cumulative learning profile should be evidence of a collaborative, longitudinal, and professional approach to assessment and evaluation of literacy acquisition.

Collaborative: Learner, peers, teacher, parents/caregivers, and administrators are active participants in the process.

Longitudinal: It is an ongoing, integrated, cumulative process of observing learning and teaching behavior.

Professional: It is responsive to philosophy and bound by the most current knowledge and theory of literacy learning. It is cognizant of individual and/or group differences and preferred styles of learning. It should be honest, trustworthy, respectful, valid, and credible.

- A cumulative profile gives a teacher the words with which to articulate a professional and meaningful account of a learner's progress and achievement.

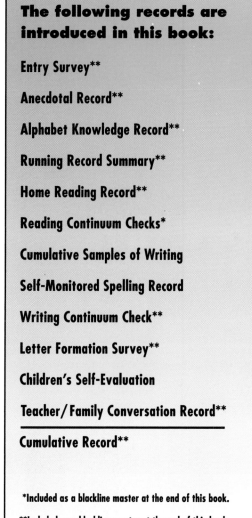

The following records are introduced in this book:

Entry Survey**

Anecdotal Record**

Alphabet Knowledge Record**

Running Record Summary**

Home Reading Record**

Reading Continuum Checks*

Cumulative Samples of Writing

Self-Monitored Spelling Record

Writing Continuum Check**

Letter Formation Survey**

Children's Self-Evaluation

Teacher/Family Conversation Record**

Cumulative Record**

*Included as a blackline master at the end of this book.

**Included as a blackline master at the end of this book and also available as a separate record pad in Rigby's Evaluation Package

The Evaluation Process

Set Learning Goals

KNOWING THE CHILDREN

KNOWING LEARNING THEORY

Evaluate

Plan Program

KNOWING ABOUT LEARNING FOR TEACHING

KNOWING LEARNING PROCESS

Assess

Observing Children 2

ASSESSMENT PROCEDURES

talking with and listening to children

conversations with parents/caregivers

conversations with colleagues

conversations with other educational agencies

observing alphabet knowledge development

observing reading development

observing writing and spelling development

observing speaking and listening development

self-evaluation

RECORDS

entry survey

anecdotal records

alphabet knowledge record

running records of text reading

running record summary

home reading record

reading continuum checks

cumulative samples of writing

self-monitored spelling record

writing continuum checks

letter formation survey

self-evaluation records

*C*hildren follow different paths to literacy, they move at different rates, and will arrive at different times. Our goal is that they *do* arrive. Sensitive and systematic observations ensure that we are constantly aware of their progress, that we support and encourage them along the way, and are there to welcome them when they arrive.

Parents are constantly watching, responding, interacting, and intervening with their children in a wide range of relevant, meaningful contexts. In the process they gather vital information on which to base their ongoing observations. This information guides their decisions about fur-

ther requirements, expectations, modifications, and goals in their everyday living.

In classrooms, teachers are the researchers and instructional decision makers. We must be ever-conscious of watching our learners very carefully and take the time to stop, look, and listen.

STOP—Stand still, watch, and listen. Reflect upon your knowledge about the developmental nature of learning and watch the social activity in front of your eyes.

LOOK—Watch closely without judgment. Articulate the precise behaviors that you see, and reflect upon the various possible intentions. Ask yourself: What does this tell me the child knows, is interested in, understands? Value what you see as a source of significant information about learning. Continue to question your own assumptions and check your own perceptions. Consider a variety of possible interpretations. Search for signals. Challenge your own thinking.

LISTEN—Hear what children are saying to each other. Hear the patterns of talk, the different roles that individual children take on during conversations, and the conditions under which this happens. Listen to the words they write, feel the imagery, and hear the music.

Observation takes place within the context of the learning environment, so noticing natural behaviors is a practice we should develop as an art. It needs to be sensitive and quick in its perception, appreciative of differences, and considerate of feelings.

Generally, teachers tend to make intuitive interpretations of the behaviors of individual children, and different teachers will see different things when observing the same behaviors. Interpretations will be affected by any particular teacher's expectations of an individual child at a given time.

These can be positive and/or negative, depending on a number of influential factors, such as context, level of interaction and engagement, and previous observations of a particular set of

Develop the habit of noticing behaviors, and value what you see and hear as a source of information to reflect on.

behaviors. They will also reflect teacher attitudes, values, knowledge and understandings about learning.

Intuitive behavior interpretations alone are unreliable as an indicator of a child's attitudes, knowledge, and competencies, unless checked and balanced with, or against, information gathered in a variety of forms and in a variety of contexts.

The Evaluation Process

Set Learning Goals

KNOWING THE CHILDREN

KNOWING LEARNING THEORY

Evaluate

KNOWING ABOUT LEARNING FOR TEACHING

Plan Program

Assess

KNOWING LEARNING PROCESS

Knowing the Children

3

ASSESSMENT PROCEDURES

watching the children

talking with and listening to children

conversations with parents/caregivers

conversations with colleagues

conversations with other educational agencies

RECORDS

entry survey

anecdotal records

Knowing the learner is central to educational assessment and evaluation. This has implications for teachers that reach out beyond the social and physical boundaries of classroom and school. It means we must make learning environments whole, relevant, and meaningful for every child who comes into our care. Knowing the learner means not only watching him/her carefully at school, but also requires that we collaborate with the children, their families, colleagues, and other appropriate educational personnel.

Begin by making the first four weeks of the school year a "getting to know you" time.

Reflect upon the kinds of information that will be most effective in helping you truly understand the children, and think about the ways in which you will help them to know you.

Begin by Asking Yourself:

- How well do I know the children?

- How can I help them to know me?

- What do I know about the sociocultural contexts of their homes—the values they live by—in order that my responses at all times are respectful, sensitive, and a demonstration of genuine interest?

- What do I know about their interests, their joys, their strengths, their fears, what they value, and care deeply about?

- How will I share with them what I value and care deeply about?

- What do I know about their pastimes—experiences in the home before they come to me and when they leave me at the end of the day, the week, the year?

- What will I share about my own pastimes, hobbies, and interests?

- Are there significant health factors that I must be aware of?

- How can I begin to find out?

ASSESSMENT PROCEDURES

Watching the Children

Develop the habit of noticing behaviors and reflecting upon what you see.

Plan to

- watch children as they interact with each other

- watch children when they choose to be alone

- notice personal preferences and choices of self-selected activities

Talking with and Listening to Children

If you want to know what children are interested in, ask them.

If you want to know how they understand something, ask them.

If you want to know how they feel about something, ask them.

Plan to

- talk informally with children in a variety of situations throughout the day

- listen to children and observe them as they talk among themselves and when they engage in group discussions

- talk with and listen to learners on a regular basis while they are reading and writing

- organize time and opportunities for children to share their responses to learning tasks—with the class, with a group, with a friend, and with you alone

Capitalize on the teachable moment. Planned conversations as children read and write, or about their reading and writing, enable the teacher to respond directly to the strengths, interests, and specific learning needs on the spot.

> *Everything you hear a child say and see a child do is a glimpse into a mind and a source of information to "know" from.*

Talking with parents will give access to very personalized information about their child, helping you to understand that child more.

Conversations with Parents/Caregivers

When children come into school and into our classrooms, we enter into a partnership with them and with their families. This means shared responsibility and the need for open and honest communication. Having a collaboratively developed agenda is a simple idea for enhancing open communication during more formal conversations with family.*

Think of innovative, appropriate ways to show parents/caregivers how the information they share with us helps us facilitate their child's learning at school. Validate their knowledge, inform them, educate them, trust them, negotiate with them, collaborate with them, and at all times demonstrate a professional interest in and caring for their child's educational progress.

Plan to

- make positive, spontaneous contact with home

- make home visits

- ensure parent inclusion

- provide written contact through
  — pamphlets for parents/caregivers
  — newsletters
  — surveys

*Teacher/Family Conversation Record included as a blackline master at the end of this book. Also available as a separate record pad in Rigby's Evaluation Package.

—school-home notebooks/
diaries/journals

—written report cards

• organize social contact through

—school events

—cultural events

—parents sharing hobbies and/or
artistic skills

—parents reading to children and
listening to children read

—fund-raising activities

Conversations with Colleagues

Talking with colleagues on an informal and/or formal basis is a useful collaborative strategy for gathering information about learners, learning, and teaching.*

Plan to meet on a regular basis to talk with each other about

• class and/or school climate and tone

• highlights or concerns about class programs in action

• management and organizational strategies

• resources and resource utilization

A word of caution here: At the beginning of a new school year, I encourage teachers to spend the first month really getting to know the children in their classes very well before seeking information from colleagues or other educational agencies, unless there are matters of health and well-being that must be known immediately. This ensures that we enter into relationships without bias or preconceived expectations.

• collaborative planning

• assessment and evaluation procedures and schedules

• analyzing samples of children's writing

• analyzing running records

• involving and communicating with parents/caregivers

Conversations with Other Educational Agencies

It can be useful to make contact with other appropriate educational agencies, such as any preschool or after-school care program the child has attended. Information gained adds to the fund of knowledge about a child.

RECORDS

Entry Survey

This is a record that provides useful background information about a child entering your class or school.

During the first weeks of the school year, as you are "getting to know" each other, collecting information through a type of entry survey will give you valuable insights into a child's background knowledge and experience.

Entry surveys created by teachers can take a variety of forms, according to the type of information considered valuable.

Depending on the format of the recording sheet,*useful information can be gathered by

- **conversations with parents/caregivers**
- **conversations with the child as he/she responds to the survey**

A

ENTRY SURVEY

Age _____ Date _____

Name _____

Languages spoken:

Preferred language:

Type of preschool attended:

Health factors:

Special interests, strengths, needs, fears:

Teacher expectations:

Parent expectations:

Family members:

General observations of adaptation to school:

Further information can be found in Highlight My Strengths in Rigby's CLPs Package.
©1993 Rigby Education • a division of Reed Publishing (USA)

May be freely copied.

B

ENTRY SURVEY
"Getting to Know Me"

Name _____

Age _____

Date _____

My name

My age

My family

_____ at

At school I like

Further information can be found in Highlight My Strengths in Rigby's CLPs Package.
©1993 Rigby Education • a division of Reed Publishing (USA)

May be freely copied.

- **cumulative responses to an interactive study about "Myself"**

C

My name is Ben... This is me. I am 5 years old. I live at ELM STREET. This is my house. Here is my family. My pets. My friends are Pablo Mark David. My hobbies. At school I like to read

*Entry Survey Records A and B are included as blackline masters at the end of this book.
Also available as separate pads in Rigby's Evaluation Package.

ANECDOTAL RECORDS

These are brief notes that record observations of actual verbal and nonverbal behaviors, and/or significant shifts in general social, emotional, and intellectual behaviors, by individual children as they interact within the learning environment. Collectively, this narrative of observed behaviors is a valuable and integral component of the assessment process. It adds an intuitive thread—a cause for consideration and reflection before judgment and action.

Why Keep Anecdotal Records?

Anecdotal notes over time help you to identify patterns and themes in learning behavior. Reflective, tentative interpretations of these behaviors give insights into a child's interests, attitudes, knowledge, learning preferences, and social relationships. We can develop our own understandings of the kind of person each child perceives himself or herself to be.

What Should Be Recorded?

Anecdotal notes record general observations of child behavior. Observe children in the playground before school, during recess, after school, in the classroom going about self-selected activities, and within the context of the program in action.

Record samplings of what you actually see a child do and/or what you hear a child say as he or she interacts within the school/classroom environment.

Sometimes you may record your interpretations of those behaviors. It is important that what you write is factual and objective, not judgmental.

Develop the skill of "eavesdropping." You can learn so much about how children make sense of their world and learn naturally—from each other, about each other, and with each other—by their conversations during play.

Your notes may include quotes from conversations, e.g.,

"I like reading the Big Books best."
What does this tell you?

"My father won't read to me 'cuz that's why he can't read."
What does this alert you to?

Develop the habit of eavesdropping on conversations. You can learn so much about how children learn naturally with—and from—each other.

Anecdotal notes should include records of general observations of reading, writing, social and/or other behaviors of interest observed within the classroom environment. They should also include notes written during specific conversations with individual children about their reading and writing on a regular basis, i.e., at least every six weeks, along with each running record taken and each sample of writing selected for the child's CLP.

Talking with Children about Their Reading

Conversations with individual children about their reading should be driven by a desire to understand how connections were made with a story idea and what the text meant to the child personally.

This means engaging in respectful, caring dialogue with the child, rather than firing a set of preselected questions to which you already know the answers, and to which the child *knows* that you know the answers. This latter approach makes the whole exercise a "test," rather than a genuine desire to understand.

Your notes would record such things as: the text read, who initiated the reading, responses to the reading, reading behaviors reinforced, specific teaching points that were addressed during the course of the conversation, etc.

Talking with children about their writing will help you to understand how they view themselves as writers, and let you gain insights into what they understand about writing and spelling.

Talking with Children about Their Writing

Conversations with individual children about something they have written is a way of showing that you are sincerely interested in the messages they are conveying, and in them personally as writers. It is a time when you can offer reflective response and individual support to children writing, while gaining insights into their knowledge and understandings about writing and the systems for conventional spelling.

Once more your notes would record such things as: who initiated the writing, the purpose for the writing, the style, the intended audience, the writer's opinion of the writing, and any specific teaching points that were addressed during the course of the conversation, etc.

Talking with Others

It is useful to keep brief notes of conversations with parents/caregivers, colleagues, and other educational personnel. Your collective recordings should include anecdotes of:

- social behavior
- health factors
- speaking and listening behaviors
- reading behaviors
- writing behaviors
- activity preferences

It is the collecting of such information *over time* that helps you gain insights into the patterns and themes of the learning behaviors and learning preferences of individual children.

The following two examples of anecdotal records,* taken with one child during her first week at school and then again at six weeks, show how this observational procedure can provide records of shifts in behavior over time, along with useful information about personal preferences, styles of learning, attitudes, interests, and potential.

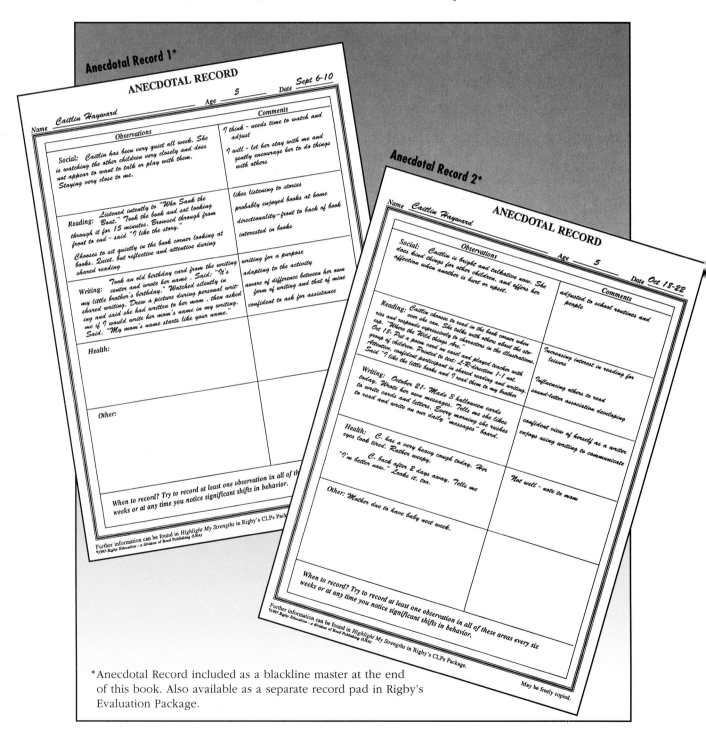

Anecdotal Record 1*

ANECDOTAL RECORD

Name _Caitlin Hayward_ Age _5_ Date _Sept 6-10_

Observations	Comments
Social: Caitlin has been very quiet all week. She is watching the other children very closely and does not appear to want to talk or play with them. Staying very close to me.	I think - needs time to watch and adjust. I will - let her stay with me and gently encourage her to do things with others
Reading: Listened intently to "Who Sank the Boat." Took the book and sat looking through it for 15 minutes. Browsed through from front to end - said "I like the story." Chooses to sit quietly in the book corner looking at books. Quiet, but reflective and attentive during shared reading	likes listening to stories probably enjoyed books at home directionality-front to back of book interested in books
Writing: Took an old birthday card from the writing center and wrote her name. Said: "It's my little brother's birthday." Watched silently in shared writing. Drew a picture during personal writing and said she had written her mom's name in my writing. Said, "My mom's name starts like your name."	writing for a purpose adapting to the activity aware of difference between her own form of writing and that of mine confident to ask for assistance
Health:	
Other:	

When to record? Try to record at least one observation in all of the weeks or at any time you notice significant shifts in behavior.

Further information can be found in *Highlight My Strengths* in Rigby's CLPs Package
©1993 Rigby Education - a division of Reed Publishing (USA)

Anecdotal Record 2*

ANECDOTAL RECORD

Name _Caitlin Hayward_ Age _5_ Date _Oct 18-22_

Observations	Comments
Social: Caitlin is bright and talkative now. She does kind things for other children, and offers her affection when another is hurt or upset.	adjusted to school routines and people
Reading: Caitlin chooses to read in the book corner when ever she can. She talks with others about the stories and responds expressively to characters in the illustrations. Oct 18- Put a poem card on easel and played teacher with group of children. Pointed to text: L-R direction 1-1 not. Attentive, confident participant in shared reading and writing. Said "I like the little books and I read them to my brother	Increasing interest in reading for leisure. Influencing others to read. sound-letter association developing
Writing: October 21- Made 3 halloween cards today. Wrote her own messages. Tells me she likes to write cards and letters. Every morning she rushes to read and write on our daily "messages" board.	confident view of herself as a writer enjoys using writing to communicate
Health: C. has a very heavy cough today. Her eyes look tired. Rather weepy. C. back after 2 days away. Tells me "I'm better now." Looks it, too.	Not well - note to mom
Other: Mother due to have baby next week.	

When to record? Try to record at least one observation in all of these areas every six weeks or at any time you notice significant shifts in behavior.

Further information can be found in *Highlight My Strengths* in Rigby's CLPs Package.
©1993 Rigby Education - a division of Reed Publishing (USA)

May be freely copied.

*Anecdotal Record included as a blackline master at the end of this book. Also available as a separate record pad in Rigby's Evaluation Package.

4 Observing Alphabet Knowledge Development

The Evaluation Process

Set Learning Goals

KNOWING THE CHILDREN

KNOWING LEARNING THEORY

Plan Program

KNOWING LEARNING PROCESS

Assess

KNOWING ABOUT LEARNING FOR TEACHING

Evaluate

Many little children come to school saying that they know "the alphabet." What we generally find is that they know a song called *The Alphabet*. They often do not know the difference between a letter and a word, or between a sound and a word, as they speak.

Within a balanced literacy program, where children actually engage in a wide range of relevant, meaningful reading and writing activities every day, they will begin to notice the differences and to develop an awareness of the relationships between sounds and letters.

You will see evidence of this growth of knowledge by looking at their writing, watching their reading and writing behavior, and noticing when children recognize letters or clusters of letters in the environment. For example, a child pointing to the word *chocolate* in a book title may say, "That begins the same as Charles."

As they express themselves through writing, children will naturally apply their knowledge of sound-symbol relationships to approximating spelling.

Shared reading and shared writing—reading with children and writing in front of children—provide powerful opportunities for demonstrating and focusing on letter-sound relationships in

ASSESSMENT PROCEDURES

- ongoing observations—noticing behaviors, as children

  —engage with environmental print, i.e., when you see or hear a child noticing/attending to letters, clusters of letters, patterns of letters in words in the environment

  —participate in shared reading, i.e., when you notice confident participation and graphophonic application to predicting and confirming words in the text

  —participate in shared writing, i.e., when you notice confident participation and frequent accurate matching of sounds to symbols when approximating spellings

- analysis of samples of writing

RECORDS

- anecdotal records
- alphabet knowledge checks at
  —6 weeks
  —6 months
  —1 year

the context of something relevant and meaningful.

Knowing the alphabet, recognizing the letters as symbolic representations of sounds, and learning to use the knowledge effectively in the process of independent reading, writing and spelling is not just left to chance.

Encouraging alphabet knowledge development, i.e., recognition of letter names, letter – sound associations, sounds in context, and seeing visual similarities and patterns in words, is an essential component of good first teaching. Careful planning will ensure that children have many opportunities to acquire this knowledge and apply it effectively in the context of their own reading and writing experiences.

The sounds and recognition of letters are best learned in the process of knowing interesting words. Develop an environment that is filled with relevant fabulous words, displayed in meaningful fabulous ways.

Where better to begin than with what is likely to be the most important word in a child's life – his or her name? Display children's names and encourage conversation about them, e.g.,

My name is Lisa.
This is how it's written.
That letter is "L."
I can hear the sound..., etc.

- Fill the day with interesting words through stories. Have fun with words: riddles, nonsense words, tongue-twisters, songs, poems.

- Set up an alphabet center, displaying
  —alphabet books, e.g., *Alison's Zinnia* (Anita Lobel) or *Farm Alphabet Book* (Jane Miller),
  —magnetic letters, with worthwhile alphabet games and activities.

- Display alphabet charts, captions, and friezes around the room.

- Play alphabet games, e.g., "I spy with my little eye..."

- Read and share poetry and rhyme books, e.g., *Bibbilibonty* (Rigby).

- In Shared Reading use lively stories, poems, and songs with repetitive use of specific letters and structures, e.g., *Fly Fly Witchy* (Rigby) – fl blend.

- In Shared Writing create innovations on texts that have repetitive use of letters, clusters of letters, patterns and rhythms in words, e.g., from *Lavender the Library Cat* (Rigby):

She saw books about stars, and books about cars.

Systematic observation of alphabet knowledge development will ensure that children who are taking longer than most to acquire this knowledge will receive small group or individualized instruction for acceleration at the appropriate time within the context of the classroom program.

USING THE ALPHABET KNOWLEDGE RECORD

Resources

- master card of alphabet letters:* photocopy the blackline master and mount on cardboard

- recording sheet**

- Allow 5-10 minutes

The alphabet letters are deliberately positioned out of alphabetical sequence.

STEP 1

- Sit beside the child.

- Give the child the master card.

- You have the alphabet knowledge recording sheet.**

- Fill in child's name, age, and date of check.

*Included as a blackline master at the end of this book.

**Alphabet Knowledge Record included as a blackline master at the end of this book. Also available as a separate record pad in Rigby's Evaluation Package.

STEP 2

- Point generally to the letters on the master card and ask, "What are these?"

STEP 3

- Say, "Would you look at each of these letters and tell me what they say? If you don't know, just go on to the next one."

- Record each correct response with a check. Count as correct those responses which include
  —alphabet letter name   ✔ Al
  —sound   ✔ Sd
  —word beginning with   ✔ word given

- Underline each letter not known or circle misidentified, i.e.,
  —no response $\underline{B}$
  —incorrect response $\widehat{B}^{M}$

STEP 4

- Record total correct.

- Note preferred mode of response, i.e., alphabet letter name, sound or word beginning with.

- Talk with child and highlight letters known—be positive.

- Make a comment on such things as
  —confidence with which the child approached the task
  —instructional implications

Taking one such alphabet knowledge check with each child in your class during the first six weeks at school will give you an overview of the level of alphabet knowledge across the whole class. This information shapes the instructional emphasis for letter recognition in your daily program. A further check at about six months will show how children have progressed and identify those who need more individualized attention at this time. At the end of the year you will be seeking to check once more the overall development of alphabet knowledge and identify children who need individualized attention to alphabet knowledge development.

Remember that

- It is not necessary that a child recognizes every letter consistently in all three categories at once.

- The purpose of this record is to observe how a child recognizes individual letters of the alphabet, how many are recognized, what individual support is needed, and what the instructional emphasis needs to be in the classroom program.

- The best observation of a child's facility with sound-symbol relationships can be seen in his/her reading and in his/her writing.

- It is useful to keep a record of the letters, letter clusters, letter blends, and repeated phrases that you have highlighted during shared writing and shared reading and be alert to reinforcing them as they arise in personal reading and writing.

- It is important to always talk about letters by alphabet name, and the sounds they make in the context of interesting words at the same time.

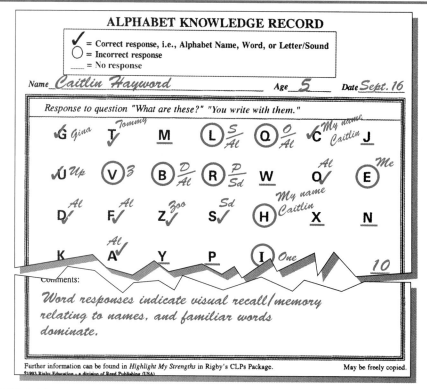

ALPHABET KNOWLEDGE RECORD

✓ = Correct response, i.e., Alphabet Name, Word, or Letter/Sound
○ = Incorrect response
___ = No response

Name _Caitlin Hayward_   Age _5_   Date _Sept. 16_

Response to question "What are these?" "You write with them."

Comments:
Word responses indicate visual recall/memory relating to names, and familiar words dominate.

Further information can be found in *Highlight My Strengths* in Rigby's CLPs Package.   May be freely copied.
©1993 Rigby Education • a division of Reed Publishing (USA)

5 Observing Reading Development

The Evaluation Process

Set Learning Goals · KNOWING THE CHILDREN · KNOWING LEARNING THEORY · Plan Program · KNOWING LEARNING PROCESS · Assess · KNOWING ABOUT LEARNING FOR TEACHING · Evaluate

Learning to read is a developmental process, and individual children will progress toward independence as readers at different rates.

Assessment procedures and records must enable the children to show *that* they are learning and *how* they are learning what it is we expect them to learn.

In a rich whole-literacy classroom environment, where children are respected and valued and where all participants actively engage in worthwhile collaborative and independent literacy activities, literate behaviors will inevitably occur.

THE STAGES OF READING DEVELOPMENT

A strategy for monitoring, organizing, and managing children learning to read in their first years at school is to consider a developmental continuum of three broad stages of development:

- *emergent stage—getting started*

- *early stage—on the way*

- *fluency stage—going it alone*

Each of the stages can be linked to both specific and general observable reading behaviors. The behaviors in

ASSESSMENT PROCEDURES

- watching children engage in self-selected, self-initiated reading activities

- conversations with children about their reading

- listening to children converse with each other about reading and writing

- noting participation in shared reading

- noticing attention and interest in listening to stories

- noticing participation in shared writing

- noticing the influence of reading in the children's spoken language, writing, and spelling development

- observing reading behaviors, both verbal and nonverbal, as a child reads from meaningful whole texts

RECORDS

- anecdotal records
- running records*
- running record summary
- home reading record
- reading continuum checks

*For further information refer to Marie Clay, *The Early Detection of Reading Difficulties* (Heinemann)

Also refer to Leanna Traill's videos, *Learning Running Records* and *Using Running Records* in the Rigby Evaluation Package.

Reading to, reading with, and reading by — essential components for readers through all stages of development.

turn can be checked and balanced against anecdotal records, running records of oral text reading, analysis of cumulative writing samples, and reading continuum checks in the process of evaluation.

Knowing what these behaviors are most likely to be will sharpen your skills in observing, interpreting and understanding learning behaviors and help you

- find out what children know, and clarify what they need to know next
- set clear learning goals and be specific about your instructional focus
- plan appropriate teaching approaches, strategies, and resources
- gather information and assess progress
- judge the effectiveness of your planning and teaching

The Emergent Stage— Getting Started

Within a rich balanced literacy environment, little children show by their behaviors that they are developing the attitudes, knowledge, and skills of readers who are "getting started," i.e., they behave like readers.

ATTITUDES

Children at the Emergent Stage

- enjoy listening to stories
- show real interest in books and environmental print
- choose to return many times to favorite books
- show interest and delight in illustrations
- retell favorite stories and rhymes
- participate confidently in shared reading
- participate confidently in shared writing
- enjoy writing by themselves
- want to take books home to read

KNOWLEDGE

Children at the Emergent Stage

- acknowledge messages, words, and letters in the environment
- understand the difference between letters and words
- understand that writers use letter symbols to form words
- can recognize some or all letters of the alphabet
- recognize and use some or all letters and words from around the classroom as a reference when writing
- understand that the print carries the message
- expect to get meaning from text
- understand that the illustrations illuminate the meaning in the text

SKILLS

Children at the Emergent Stage

- can show the front cover/back cover/spine of a book
- have established L-R directional movement on one line of text
- have established L-R directional movement on more than one line of text
- match and check 1-1 correspondence
- use illustrations as a clue to challenges in the text
- can indicate a word/letter
- recognize some high-frequency words out of context
- can spell some high-frequency words accurately

This list of behaviors guides the selection of learning goals and instructional decisions for emergent readers and can be balanced against the Emergent Reading Continuum Check.*

*Included as a blackline master at the end of this book.

The Early Stage—On the Way

Readers at the early stage will show that they are "on the way" by their increasing confidence, knowledge, skills, and understandings on more complex texts.

ATTITUDES

Children at the Early Stage

- enjoy listening to longer stories

- return to favorite books

- choose to read independently

- expect to get meaning from text

- respond to meaning in text by relating to prior experience

- choose to explore unfamiliar resources

- take initiative for responding creatively to books

- are confident to share feelings about books

- participate confidently in shared reading

- participate confidently in shared writing

KNOWLEDGE

Children at the Early Stage

- reread words, lines, and paragraphs to check meaning

- bring own knowledge of oral and written language to reading

- are developing increased knowledge of conventions of print

- take responsibility for selecting words for personal spelling lists

- are less reliant on illustrations as a clue to making meaning in text

- know how written text works, e.g., directional conventions

- understand the concepts of letter, word, sentence

- are consolidating sound-symbol relationships

- recognize simple punctuation conventions

SKILLS

Children at the Early Stage

- are beginning to integrate language cues effectively

- are beginning to monitor their own reading by cross-checking a number of meaning-making strategies when reading, e.g., the child checks predictions made on the basis of semantic and syntactic cues by looking at letters and clusters of letters (attending to graphophonic cues)

- are demonstrating strategies for coping with challenges in text

- are developing ability to retell longer stories in sequence

- are developing ability to recall facts from informational books

- write with confidence and enthusiasm

- begin to demonstrate the influence of the authors they read in their personal writing

This list of behaviors guides the selection of learning goals and instructional decisions for early readers and can be balanced against the Early Reading Continuum Check.*

The Fluency Stage— Going It Alone

Children at the fluency stage will exhibit the behaviors of mature readers and writers. They will

- read silently for leisure, pleasure, and information

- choose to read independently from an increasing variety of genres for a variety of purposes

- enjoy listening to chapter-book stories as well as picture books

- read chapter books and nonfiction informational texts of particular interest

- expect to have independent control of first reading of an unseen text

- take initiative in responding to books

- become more critical and reflective about the messages and information in text

- demonstrate confidence in using the strategies for predicting, sampling, confirming, and/or self-correcting when engaging with an unfamiliar text

Fluent readers confidently choose from a wide range of genres when reading for leisure, pleasure, and information.

- expect challenges—and handle them with confidence

- automatically call on a number of strategies when coping with challenges in text

- write with confidence and enthusiasm

- proofread writing and show increased knowledge of systems for conventional spellings

- demonstrate a growing understanding of writing in different registers for different purposes

This list of behaviors** indicates that the child is now a confident independent reader, ready to go on reading to learn and using reading and writing as tools for learning.

*Included as a blackline master at the end of this book.
**Refer to the Fluent Reading Continuum Check, included as a blackline master at the end of this book.

The following diagram shows how the planning and evaluation processes are inter-dependent, one with the other. It uses a sampling of learning goals from a weekly plan for emergent readers.

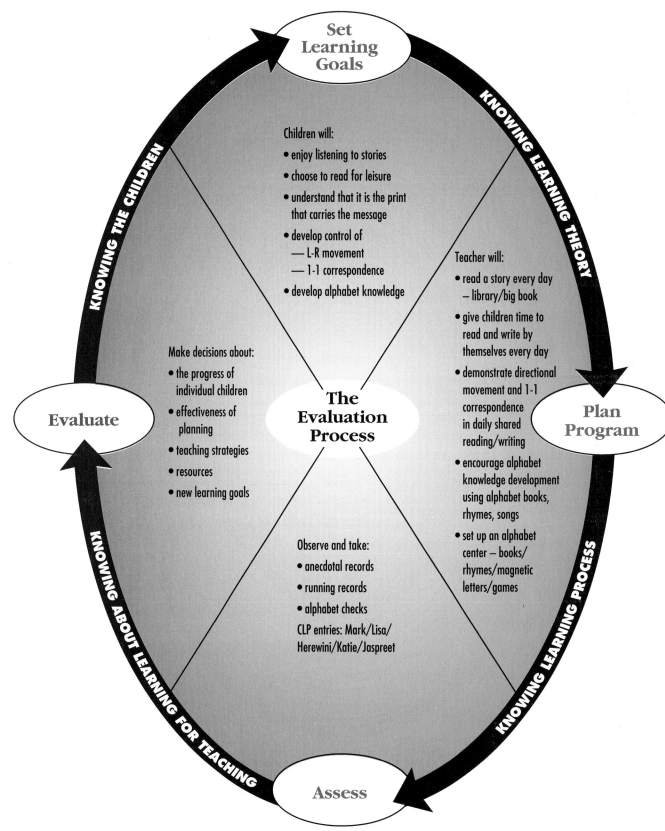

Set Learning Goals

Children will:
- enjoy listening to stories
- choose to read for leisure
- understand that it is the print that carries the message
- develop control of
  — L-R movement
  — 1-1 correspondence
- develop alphabet knowledge

KNOWING THE CHILDREN

KNOWING LEARNING THEORY

Evaluate

Make decisions about:
- the progress of individual children
- effectiveness of planning
- teaching strategies
- resources
- new learning goals

The Evaluation Process

Plan Program

Teacher will:
- read a story every day — library/big book
- give children time to read and write by themselves every day
- demonstrate directional movement and 1-1 correspondence in daily shared reading/writing
- encourage alphabet knowledge development using alphabet books, rhymes, songs
- set up an alphabet center — books/rhymes/magnetic letters/games

Observe and take:
- anecdotal records
- running records
- alphabet checks
CLP entries: Mark/Lisa/Herewini/Katie/Jaspreet

KNOWING ABOUT LEARNING FOR TEACHING

KNOWING LEARNING PROCESS

Assess

KEEPING RECORDS OF READING DEVELOPMENT

As children progress through the developmental stages of learning to read, informal observations, anecdotal records, home reading records and running records* of oral text reading provide valuable information with which to monitor

- attitudes to reading and view of self as a reader

- development of knowledge and understanding of concepts about print

- use and integration of language cues

- development and consolidation of reading strategies

- development of self-monitoring strategies

- the flexible grouping of children for guided instruction

- the selection of what teaching strategies and approaches should be used

- the selection and matching of books with children

- the need for early intervention and/or acceleration

*Marie Clay, *An Observation Survey of Early Literacy Achievement* (Heinemann).

Effective readers draw on three main cueing systems for predicting meaning in text. They integrate and cross-check their knowledge of the world around them, their knowledge of the structures of spoken language, and their knowledge of the alphabet, i.e., sound-symbol relationships, and ability to see visual similarities and patterns in words.

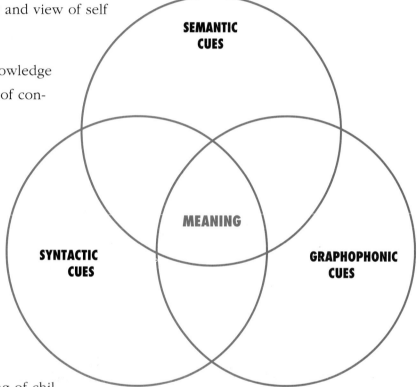

*When analyzing reading behavior ask yourself the following questions:

- Is the child trying to make sense of what is being read? (semantic cues)

- Is knowledge of language patterns being used? (syntactic cues)

- Is knowledge of letters and their associated sounds being used? (graphophonic)

- Are confirmation and self-correction strategies evident?

Develop the habit of noticing reading behaviors and reflecting on these as glimpses into how a child is developing control of the reading process. Confirm your intuitive understandings with thoughtful analysis of records of reading behaviors.

Remember that "reading for meaning is paramount." Focus on how children show you that they understand this.

Record of Oral Text Reading

Developed by Dr. Marie Clay,* this technique for recording reading behavior is the most insightful, informative, and instructionally useful assessment procedure you can use for monitoring a child's progress in learning to read.

As an ongoing, systematic component of assessment, running records have significant positive impact on a teacher's

- skill in sensitive observation and interpretation of reading behavior

- focus on what children know about reading

- knowledge of how children learn to read

- ability to identify and address the particular needs of individual children at the right time and in the right way

- skill in matching books with the instructional needs of children

- facility to articulate a professional account of a learner's progress and achievement

Running records of reading behavior can be taken on a variety of texts, though more often they are taken on texts used for guided reading within the stage through which the child is currently progressing.

* Refer to Marie Clay, *An Observation Survey of Early Literacy Achievement* (Heinemann).

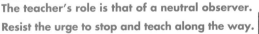

The teacher's role is that of a neutral observer. Resist the urge to stop and teach along the way.

Texts used can be those that are seen (familiar) or unseen (unfamiliar). In the context of this book and the two videos on running records,* *Learning Running Records and Using Running Records,* **seen** and **unseen** are defined as

seen - *has been read independently by the child before*

unseen - *has not been read independently by the child before*

Texts the reader has enjoyed in shared reading with the whole class but has not yet read independently would still be recorded as **unseen**. When a text has **never** been seen or heard by a child, there should always be a brief orientation prior to the first reading.

Remember that any technique for observing reading behavior must return instructionally useful information. The more familiar the text, the less information you will receive.

Establish a systematic schedule for ensuring that a running record is taken with each child on a regular basis. While you may aim to do this every six weeks, it is extremely useful to take them more frequently with readers at the emergent and early stages.

Texts	Recording Schedule
emergent stage	
dictated text	at least one running record with every child every 6 weeks
poem card	more often with children you need to monitor more closely
published personal or shared writing	
guided reading text	
early stage	
poem card	one running record with every child every 6 weeks
big book text	more often with children you need to monitor more closely
published shared writing	
guided reading text	
fluency stage	
a selection from literature	one running record with every child at the beginning, middle, and end of year
a selection of paragraphs from a guided reading text	with a newcomer on entry to the class to find out how a child is reading
sampling from a nonfiction text	more frequently with a child who changes in attitude and confidence and begins to experience difficulty with reading
informal prose inventory of passages not previously read by the reader	

*Leanna Traill's videos are available in Rigby's Evaluation Package.

The following examples of records of reading behavior show how informative and instructionally useful this observational technique can be.

Example 1: The Emergent Stage—first week at school

Text: Dictated/Painting

Here are three typical outcomes of running records taken during the first week of a school year, as five-year-olds read a dictated text. The text is accepted and written as it was given. You will notice that even at this very emergent stage, each of the records provides useful information about what a child knows about reading, and shows progress toward the learning goals set for emergent readers. (See page 25.)

My cat goed up the tree and it got stuck.

✓ ✓ goed up

goed up the tree and

the tree and it

it ✓ ✓

got . Pointed and

said, "That's the end."

✓ ✓ ✓ ✓

✓ ✓ ✓ ✓

✓ ✓

Said, "My dad got it down with the ladder."

Pointed to stuck: "That word starts like Steven."

Pointed to the: "That says 'the'."

ANALYSIS	INSTRUCTIONAL DECISIONS

Simply pointed to where the text is and tapped out the rhythm as she recited the sentence

Understands that it is the print that carries the message

Confident, positive approach

Needs

ongoing shared reading/writing

time to read and write independently every day

encouragement to point to the words when reading

Understands

    the print carries the message

    where to start reading

    direction L-R, L-R and return

    the use of a period

1-1 correspondence not yet established

Happy, confident approach

Needs

encouragement to attend to 1-1

ask her to point when reading with me

demonstrations of matching 1-1 through shared reading/writing

opportunities to match cut-up sentences on rhyme cards

Accurate reading

    L-R, and L-R and return

    1-1 firmly established

    voiced and finger pointed as she read

Beginning to recognize the similarities in words, and to identify high-frequency words

Confident, positive atitude

Needs

reinforcement of this self-monitoring behavior—encourage reading, but at a more natural pace—model to show her, clap the rhythm

reinforce and encourage her attention to the similarities among letters and clusters of letters in words

Example 2: The Emergent Stage—4 months at school

Text: *Dressing Up, Literacy 2000,* Stage 1

This example shows a reader progressing through the emergent stage of learning to read. Knowledge and understandings of concepts about print* are evident, and reading strategies are developing. (Refer page 25.)

You will note that the repetitive structure and the consistent placement of the text provide support for the reader until the last page, where the structure changes, and the increased text challenges her confidence. There are times, often at the emergent and early stages, when the accuracy rating can be incidental to the instructional decisions you make.

For example, the rating in this record was affected by the reader's repetitive insertion of the word *a*, and repetitive omission of word endings. The record of behaviors and the analysis of errors, however, indicate that the child was confidently reading the text with full understanding; therefore the accuracy rating in this case becomes incidental.

*Marie Clay, *An Observation Survey of Early Literacy Achievement* (Heinemann).

RUNNING RECORD*

Name _Katie_   Age _5.4_   Date _10-21-91_

Title/Text _Dressing Up_   Emergent ☑   Early ☐   Fluent ☐   Seen ☐ Unseen ☑

Running Words (RW) _33_ Errors (E) _14_ Error Rate (ER) _1:2.5_		
Self-Corrections (SC) _—_ Self-Correction Rate (SCR) _—_ %Accuracy (ACC) _55_		

Easy ☐   Instructional ☐   Too Challenging ☑
(Key for scoring a running record on back of this sheet)

M	Meaning (Semantic)
S	Structure (Syntactic)
V	Visual (Graphophonic)

Analysis of Errors: _Using meaning and structure cues, but tending to ignore visual. Not attending to 1-1 correspondence—this still developing._

Summary: _Katie is reading for meaning. Uses the illustrations for clues to the text. L-R established. Encourage to point when reading. Continue to demonstrate 1-1 in shared reading/writing_

Page Number					# of E	# of SC	Error Analysis	Self-Correction Analysis
T.P.	✓	✓						
2	The |||| ✓ They |T	✓		a dress — dresses	3		Ⓜ Ⓢ Ⓥ Ⓜ Ⓢ v Ⓜ Ⓢ Ⓥ	
3	✓	✓	✓	a coat — coats	2		Ⓜ Ⓢ v Ⓜ Ⓢ Ⓥ	
4	✓	✓	✓	a hat — hats	2		Ⓜ Ⓢ v Ⓜ Ⓢ Ⓥ	
5	✓	✓	✓	✓				
6	✓	✓	✓	necklace beads	1		Ⓜ Ⓢ v	
7	↓✓	✓	✓	lip | R/✓ lipstick				
8	They go|| go And they went ✓	Miss Browns visit Mrs. Brown			3 3		Ⓜ Ⓢ v Ⓜ Ⓢ v Ⓜ S v Ⓜ Ⓢ v Ⓜ Ⓢ v Ⓜ Ⓢ Ⓥ	

* Form adapted from Marie Clay, _An Observation Survey of Early Literacy Achievement_ (Heinemann).

Example 3: The Early Stage— 1 year at school

Text: *Ask Nicely*, **Literacy 2000**, Stage 3

This record is evidence of the progress from the emergent stage through to the early stage. Early strategies and reading behaviors are now maintained on longer, more challenging texts.

This example of a running record has been set out this way to show the process

---

RUNNING RECORD

Name *Jaspreet* Age *6.4* Date *3-6-91*

Title/Text *Ask Nicely* Emergent ☐ Early ☑ Fluent ☐ Seen ☑ Unseen ☐

Running Words (RW) *///* Errors (E) *7* Error Rate (ER) *1:15*

Self-Corrections (SC) *3* Self-Correction Rate (SCR) *1:3* %Accuracy (ACC) *93*

Easy ☐ Instructional ☑ Too Challenging ☐
(Key for scoring a running record on back of this sheet)

M	Meaning (Semantic)
S	Structure (Syntactic)
V	Visual (Graphophonic)

Analysis of Errors: *Integrating all language cues effectively. Tending to ignore closer visual checking of structural detail in words. Her control of English language overrides the need for closer visual checking.*

Summary: *Jaspreet is reading for meaning with confidence. She is developing strategies for monitoring her own reading. Needs encouragement to attend to structural analysis of words when reading. Learning to read in her second language.*

	Page Number		# of E	# of SC	Error Analysis	Self-Correction Analysis
Ask Nicely	T.P.	✓ ✓				
The giant was angry. "Come here!" he roared. "No way!" said the grocer.	2/3	✓ ✓ ✓ ✓ / ✓ ✓ ✓ ✓ / ✓ ✓ ✓ ✓ butcher/grocer	1		M (S) v	
The giant shook his fist. "Come here!" he roared. "No way!" said the butcher.	4/5	✓ ✓ stop•T/shook ✓ feet/fist / ✓ ✓ ✓ ✓ / ✓ ✓ ✓ ✓ ✓	2		M (S)(V) / M (S)(V)	
The giant stamped his foot. "Come here!" he roared. "No way!" said the baker.	6/7	✓ ✓ ✓ ✓ feet/foot / ✓ ✓ ✓ ✓ / ✓ ✓ ✓ ✓ ✓	1		M (S)(V)	
The giant yelled and howled. "Come here! COME HERE! There's a prickle in my toe! Someone get it out!"	8/9	There/sc ✓ yell/yelled ✓ howl/howled / The✓ ✓ ✓ yelled ✓ howled / There/There's ✓ ✓ ✓ ✓ ✓ / ✓ ✓ ✓	2 / 1	1	M (S)(V) / M (S)(V) / M (S)(V) / M (S)(V)	M S (V)
The giant began to cry. "Silly giant!" said a boy. "Why don't you ask nicely?"	10/11	M S S ✓/silly ✓ ✓ ✓ / ✓ ✓ ✓ ✓ ✓ / ✓ ✓ ✓ ✓ ✓				
The giant remembered his manners. "Come here, **please**," he said. "OK," said the boy.	12/13	✓ ✓ ✓ / ✓ ✓ / ✓ ✓ ✓ ✓ ✓ / ✓ ✓ ✓ ✓				
The giant was happy. "Thank you," he said. "My toe feels better now."	14/15	✓ R ✓ ✓/That/R ✓ said/R/SC ✓ / Thank ✓ he ✓ ✓		2	M (S)(V) / M (S) v	M(S)(V) / M(S)(V)
And he never forgot his manners again.	16	✓ ✓ ✓ ✓ / ✓ ✓ ✓				

---

of interpreting a record, and to highlight the amount of positive, instructionally useful information that can be accessed through using this assessment procedure.

Close analysis of errors and self-corrections shows clearly what Jaspreet knows and understands about the reading process, and there are clear indications of what instructional decisions need to be made for her.

These are examples of the kinds of questions you might ask yourself as you analyze each error and each self-correction:

What made Jaspreet say that/do that?

What does this tell me she knows?

What reading strategies are being used/not used?

What cues are being used/not used?*

Is she reading for meaning?

*Circle only the cues used

Analysis Interpretation	Instructional Decisions
Reading for meaning Ⓜ Structurally acceptable substitution Ⓢ Did not check visual detail Ⓥ	Jaspreet needs encouragement to attend to structural details in words, as she reads. In this text you could say, for example, "Jaspreet, on page 8 you said, 'The giant yell and howl.' Let's look at that page together. Let's look at those words." If she does not note that she omitted the endings, point out the ed endings and read the sentence clearly to her so that she can hear the ed sound. You may wish to very quickly demonstrate further by writing yell and then adding ed, or by using magnetic letters to make the word and add the ending.
Reading for meaning Ⓜ Structurally acceptable substitution Ⓢ Visually similiar, but neglected to check detail Ⓥ	
It makes sense Ⓜ Reading for meaning Ⓜ We can say it that way Ⓢ It looks right Ⓥ Not attending to close visual detail of medial letters	
SC = checking behavior evident—used Ⓥ, and likely memory, for correcting this high-frequency word Omission of endings—acceptable language to her Not attending to close visual detail in words.	Reinforce checking behavior. Focus on structural analysis of words in context of shared reading, shared writing, and when talking with her about her own reading and writing.
Used initial consonant to attempt challenging word Understands that this is a useful strategy when a word is challenging	Reinforce sounding out of the I/C (initial consonant) as a useful strategy for coping with a challenging word.
	Reinforce rerun/repetition behavior as a cross-checking strategy.
Reran when she became confused (a self-monitoring strategy) intergrated all language cues for SC Ⓜ Ⓢ Ⓥ	

TAKE HOME READING RECORD*

The inclusion of family in a child's literacy development is crucial and must be conscientiously encouraged. A very positive strategy for involving family in their child's reading development is to send a book home with the child every night to share. This process has the effect of

- affirming the family role in the child's literacy development

- helping the family to understand how children learn to read and how reading is taught in school

- creating opportunities for ongoing dialogue between home and school

- setting the scene for teachers to invite parents to school to share ideas for helping their children with reading at home

The Home Reading Record is merely a record of the books a child has taken home to read. This is kept in the child's individual "Take Home" book bag, folder, or pocket, and later copied to add to the CLP.

HOME READING RECORD

Name _____   Grade _____

Date	Title	✓Read to child	✓Read with child	✓Read by child	Comments	Initials
10/12	When I Play		✓	✓	She seemed to get mixed up about the direction of the words. I helped her to point. Great. Keep doing that.	
10/15	Buffy			✓	She loves this. More secure with 1-1 pointing.	
10/17	The Selfish Giant	✓			Our favorite.	

*Home Reading Record included as a blackline master at the end of this book. Also available as a separate record pad in Rigby's Evaluation Package.

Books for reading at home can be chosen from a selection of those which can be read to the child, by the child, and/or with the child.

BOOKS FOR HOME READING

The books that are taken home to read are usually those the child knows how to read independently. They can be selected from collections of books that the child can read independently, and/or the child may choose the book taken to fluency in a guided reading session that day. In addition, there will be books that a child may have heard many times, but is not yet able to read fluently. These are also appropriate for home reading.

It is not always possible for a teacher to oversee the selection of individual books for every child every day, so the children must be shown how to do this for themselves.

The family must be well-informed as to how the books are selected, to avoid undue concern should a child not be able to read every word accurately. A useful strategy is to prepare a selection of bookmarks* (strips of cardboard will do) that go home with each book.

When the children choose their home reading book independent of the teacher, they also select the appropriate bookmark. Some children may select the same book many times. When the choice is theirs, this should be accepted and respected.

*Class sets of bookmarks are provided in Rigby's Evaluation Package.

Taking books home to read affirms the family's role in their child's reading development.

GETTING HOME READING STARTED

All parents/caregivers want their children to learn how to read. Not all parents/caregivers know *how* to help or *believe they are able* to help their children to do this. A home reading program is a positive way to show parents/caregivers how they can indeed help. Begin by

- talking with the children about home reading

- talking with parents/caregivers

- talking with older brothers and sisters at school

- writing a letter to the family, explaining the purposes and organization of home reading and requesting their support

Arrange for parents/caregivers:

- open days to visit and observe reading at school

- specific demonstrations of shared reading to show them how to support their child's reading at home

- time to explain the home reading record. Emphasize recording a brief description of the child's response. See the example on page 38.

It is important that parents/caregivers are encouraged to remain positive and supportive when listening to their child read. Emphasis on correctness may discourage the child from wanting to read and undermine his/her confidence.

The following example of a letter to family is a positive approach toward involving them in their child's reading at home.

LETTER TO FAMILY

Dear Family,

Today I am bringing a book home from school. I can keep it for one week, or I can take it back just as soon as I am finished with it. I might bring a different book home every night.

Inside the book I have placed a bookmark, which tells you how I would like to read it at home. Sometimes I'll want to read the book **all by myself**, sometimes I'll ask you to **read it with me**, and sometimes I'll ask you to **read it to me**.

When I read the book **all by myself**, listen to me read it to you right through. When I ask you to **read it with me**, let me try it first all by myself, and if I find the words too difficult, join in and read it with me. When I ask you to **read it to me**, you will know that it's a story that I really want to hear, but can't yet read by myself.

Here are some ways you can help me with my reading at home.
- Make sure we have a special "home reading" time every day.
- Read me a story or some poems or a letter every day.
- Listen to me read something every day.

When I come to a word I don't know:
- wait for awhile and let me think about it.
- remind me to look at the picture for a clue.
- suggest that I look at the first letter, then read the line again and make a guess.
- if I still can't get it, TELL ME. I'll remember it next time.

When I've/we've finished reading, let's talk about it. You might ask me what I did or didn't like about it, and you could tell me what you thought of the story. You might also talk about the illustrations or help me notice how interesting words are spelled.

Listening to you read and having you listen to me helps me to:
- love reading even more.
- learn how to read and write.
- learn about spelling.
- understand how language works.

In my "Home Reading Carrier," you'll find a record sheet. It is helpful to my teacher if you and I can show her/him how we shared the book together, and comment on the special things we talked about.

Finally, I may need you to remind me how to care for my book and return it to school so that someone else can have a turn at reading it with their family too.

Thank you for helping me. I think it's lots of fun reading with you.

Love from,

The Evaluation Process

Set Learning Goals

KNOWING THE CHILDREN

KNOWING LEARNING THEORY

Evaluate

Plan Program

KNOWING ABOUT LEARNING FOR TEACHING

Assess

KNOWING LEARNING PROCESS

Observing Writing and Spelling Development

ASSESSMENT PROCEDURES — WRITING

watching children actually writing

observing writing behaviors

talking with and listening to children talk about their writing

listening to children talk with each other about their writing

careful analysis of cumulative samples of writing

RECORDS

anecdotal records

samples of writing

letter formation survey

self-monitored spelling record

writing continuum check

ASSESSMENT PROCEDURES — SPELLING

observing spelling behaviors

observing proofreading behaviors

noticing the strategies used to spell words

observing how children approach the task of approximating spelling

hearing what they say and seeing where they go for help

close analysis of every spelling approximation throughout cumulative samples of writing

A s it is with learning to talk and learning to read, it is now well recognized that learning to write and learning systems for conventional spellings are developmental language processes. They are active, expressive, and constructive; shaped by functional, social, and contextual purpose.

Children learn to write by reading, speaking, listening, and writing. They learn more about writing every time they write independently of the teacher. Writing development must be assessed in the context of personal writing.

Children will learn to spell through reading, speaking, listening, and writing. The more chil-dren read and write, the more words they will read and spell accurately. Spelling development must be assessed in the context of personal writing.

Our goals for children learning to write and learning to spell through the early stages of development toward independence are to:

• develop and maintain a desire to write

• develop and maintain each child's view of himself/herself as a writer

• show children the strategies that writers employ as they write, as they spell, and as they proofread their writing

- help children to learn how to proofread writing and to understand the difference between this and other reading

- develop and consolidate concepts about print

- develop knowledge of sound-symbol relationships

- encourage and respond to approximated spellings

- develop correct directional formation of letters when writing

COLLECTING SAMPLES OF CHILDREN'S WRITING

Close analysis of cumulative samples of children's writing is the most effective procedure for monitoring writing and spelling development that a teacher can use. As a systematic, ongoing component of assessment, these samples

- provide authentic data on which to assess progress

- show what a child knows about the processes of writing and spelling

- help identify particular strengths and instructional needs of individual children

- influence instructional decisions, selection of resources, and teaching strategies

The concept of ownership by the writer is vital. Monitoring writing and spelling development is a sensitive process. Attention to structures of lan-

guage and approximated spellings comes after attention and response to the messages imbedded in the writing.

The decision to intervene on spelling approximations must be based on your knowledge of the child's confidence as a writer and on the child's personal readiness to participate in the analysis, explanation, and correction of his/her own spellings.

Remember when talking with a child about spelling approximations that you are searching to understand what strategies a child was using to produce the particular spelling. Your first action is to put the responsibility for any correction back on the child, before offering reflective assistance.

Recording Schedule

Establish a schedule for collecting samples of writing by individual children on a regular basis. Aim to:

- collect at least one sample every 6 weeks

- keep a sample of any writing that shows a sudden, significant shift in development

- encourage each child to select a piece of writing to add to his or her cumulative learning profile on a regular basis

- maintain ongoing dialogue with each child about his/her own writing and spelling development

- ensure children talk with each other on a daily basis about writing and, inevitably, spelling

As with every record you take and keep, writing samples must be thoughtfully analyzed and dated. It is the dating that shows the pace of progress over time.

Add a comment on:

- the context within which the writing evolved

- who initiated the purpose

- the level of independence

- the level of participation if it was a shared response

- what assistance was sought and received from others

- what sources of spelling reference were used

For example, look closely at this child's writing sample, read the following analysis and note how this shaped the instructional decisions.

Analysis:

- spelling at the phonetic stage

- writing was self-initiated: When sharing the writing, she said, "I like rainbows 'cause they are pretty colors. My cat likes them too." We focused on the word *rainbow*: compound word, gave conventional spelling.

- wrote independently, with casual discussion with friends about spellings

- enunciated words and applied sound-symbol knowledge

- insecure directionality: *b/d*

- referred to color words in personal spelling record and copied "oringe" from the walls

Instructional decisions:

- Reinforce observed learning behavior that should be encouraged.

- Continue to demonstrate sound-symbol relationships in shared reading and shared writing.

- Demonstrate and encourage attention to punctuation.

- Watch *b/d* reversal—demonstrate the difference, draw her attention to reversal.

- Reinforce compound words in shared reading and shared writing.

the raBO is ov
the cat
PoPil ahb yolo
ahb oringe
red ahb blo

The seals were swimming in the
water and one is on the rocks the
father one was singing then the other
ones began to sing.

Sometimes we read, all snuggled tight.

A B C D I F L H I C K I m o p q
R S t W V W X W S

I went out by my house too go woc for a wynday and I stopt cos I sawn hegcb eey I

STAGES OF WRITING AND SPELLING DEVELOPMENT

When analyzing samples of children's writing, knowing what to look for and respond to, and knowing how to interpret what you see, will help you follow individual children's learning progress effectively and make appropriate instructional decisions.

Documented research* has identified five developmental stages in both learning to write and learning to spell. These can be used as a starting point or guide for looking at writing and spelling development.

The stages can also be loosely paralleled with the three broad stages of reading development: emergent, early, and fluency.

Remember that children will pass through any stages of learning at different rates and at different times. They may miss out a stage altogether. The effectiveness of teacher observation, demonstration, intervention, and encouragement will impact on the rate of progress individual children make through the various stages.

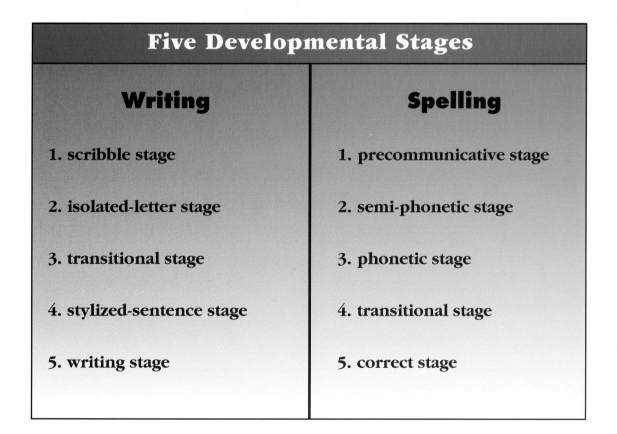

Five Developmental Stages

Writing	Spelling
1. scribble stage	1. precommunicative stage
2. isolated-letter stage	2. semi-phonetic stage
3. transitional stage	3. phonetic stage
4. stylized-sentence stage	4. transitional stage
5. writing stage	5. correct stage

*J. Richard Gentry, *Spel Is a Four-Letter Word* (Heinemann);
 John E. Heenam, *Writing: Process and Product* (Longman Paul).

THE STAGES OF WRITING

1. Scribble Stage

No recognizable letters. Writing is represented as lines, scribbles, and scrawls. The writer can "read" the scribble, but there are no clues to meaning that hold over time.

I went up North to see my Papa.

2. Isolated Letter Stage

Letters begin to appear, usually strung together, along with symbols and sometimes numbers. There continues to be an understanding of the purpose for writing. There will often be little drawings in the writing, and these help the writer hold the meaning and read back over time.

The seals were swimming in the water and one is on the rocks. The father one was singing then the other ones began to sing.

3. Transitional Stage

Some conventionally spelled words are used correctly, often at the beginning; then the writing returns to isolated letters, symbols, and numerals. Drawings continue to hold the meaning over time. This transitional stage may pass very quickly and often go unnoticed.

4. Stylized Sentence Stage

A writer will stylize sentences around known words, repetitive phrases, and sentence beginnings, using words from the environment to complete the sentences. The writing itself now provides the clues which enable the writer to read the message back over time. If writers are observed to rest in this stage, there is a need to review the quality of book resources and the effectiveness of teaching strategies.*

5. Writing Stage

Writers write freely, creatively, and independently, using both approximated spelling and conventional spelling. At this stage, the writer's voice emerges and concern for the expression of ideas is evident.

Children will write like the authors they read. The impact of reading will impact on the output of writing.

THE STAGES OF SPELLING

1. Precommunicative Stage

- developing knowledge of alphabet, evident by the use of some letter forms to represent the message

- little or no knowledge of sound-symbol relationships evident—random stringing together of letters, sometimes mixed with numbers

- may/may not show understanding of L-R directional principle

- sometimes repetitive use of a few known alphabet symbols, producing long lists

of letters of the alphabet—more often shows a preference for uppercase letters

2. Semi-phonetic Stage

- begins to attempt to represent sound-symbol correspondence

- begins to conceptualize that letters have sounds that are used to represent the whole word, e.g., skl=school

- a letter-name strategy is very much in evidence—the children represent words, sounds, or syllables with the letters that match their letter names, e.g., c=see, y=why

- L-R sequential arrangements of letters in words shows developing ability to hear sounds in sequence in words

- alphabet knowledge and mastery of letter formation is developing

- spacing of words may/may not be consistent or consolidated

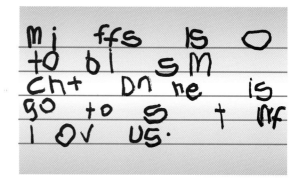

Instructional Decisions: In daily Shared Writing provide meaningful demonstrations of writing and spelling strategies. Give a high priority to the development of alphabet knowledge, awareness of sound-symbol relationships, strategies for hearing sounds in sequence in words, and concepts about print. Foster confidence and desire to write.

3. Phonetic Stage

- Represents the entire sound structure of a word

- shows evidence of total mapping of sound-letter correspondence

- shows consistent L-R orientation and word spacing

- frequently assigns letters strictly on the basis of sound, without regard for appropriate letter sequence, e.g., *stopt=stopped*

Instructional Decisions: In Shared Writing/Reading the instructional focus now shifts towards sentence structure, word analysis, and punctuation in context. Demonstrate the purpose, process, and skills for proofreading. Demonstrate the use of a variety of reference sources for conventional spellings, and beginning personal *Words I Can Almost Spell* notebooks. (Each child selects any number of approximated spellings from a sample of writing, and the teacher models the conventional spelling in a personalized notebook.)

4. Transitional Stage

- shows evidence of a transition from reliance on sound for representing words to a much greater reliance on visual representation

- begins to insert vowels in every syllable, e.g., *tayol*, instead of the phonetic *tal* (tail)

- includes all the appropriate letters, but positioning may be reversed, e.g., *hores (horse)*

- uses learned words in great abundance, and approximations show a tendency toward visual memory for spellings, e.g., *caem (came)*

Instructional Decisions: Previous teaching strategies are continued, with more emphasis on developing the habit of and skills for proofreading, encouraging paired and small group conversations about writing and spelling, reinforcing strategies for achieving conventional spellings, developing dictionary skills and wider use of other spelling references.

5. Correct Stage

- shows that the basis of knowledge of systems for conventional spelling is now firmly set. Continuing experiences with proofreading, writing, and thinking about spelling result in finer discrimination and extension of knowledge, i.e., children will learn more about spelling by reading, writing, and thinking about spelling

- uses an accumulation of a large body of known words
- displays a growing accuracy in using silent consonants and doubling consonants
- shows understanding of irregular spellings
- utilizes extended knowledge of word structures, prefixes, suffixes, contractions, and compound words

My cat   is   a Siamese cat!
I Love her   she's cute!
her   eyes glow Maroon in the
dark and her colours are caum
and   braun   with
black up her tail she has
a really cute! face !!

IMPLICATIONS FOR WRITING AND SPELLING INSTRUCTION

For children learning to write, learning to spell, and learning to use writing as a tool for learning, there are certain environmental conditions that should exist in every classroom.

Within this context, analysis of cumulative samples of writing shapes and guides instructional decisions and teaching strategies, both for individual children and for the class as a whole.

The Physical Environment:

- Develop a print-saturated environment.

- Children are surrounded by many forms of writing for many relevant and meaningful purposes.

- Provide access to many books for many purposes.

- Resources and tools for writing are readily available.

The Emotional Environment:

- Children want to write, and believe in themselves as writers.

- There is trust in and support for every child as a writer.

- There is the highest expectation that every child will learn to write and to spell by reading and writing.

- Children receive positive and constructive responses to their writing and spelling.

- The focus is first on the *message* embedded in the writing, before the structure and form of the writing.

The Intellectual Environment:

- Writing is valued in the environment.

- Reading and writing are integrated throughout the curriculum.

- Children read and write every day in a variety of relevant and meaningful contexts.

- The teacher writes in front of the children every day, providing demonstrations of the strategies that writers employ as they write, as they spell, and as they proofread writing.

- The teacher provides demonstrations of writing in a variety of forms for a variety of purposes.

- The teacher reads to and with the children every day, attending to structures of language and words in context.

Remember that:

- The input of reading will impact on the output of writing.

- Children learn to spell by reading and writing.

- They learn about spelling by talking about words in reading, writing, and spelling.

- Conversations with children about their own writing and spellings will help you to understand what they know about the two processes and what you need to encourage next.

- The children must be actively involved in evaluating their own progress in writing and spelling.

SELF-MONITORED SPELLING RECORD

This is one way of giving children responsibility for recording their own progress in achieving conventional spellings of high-frequency words.

Create a sheet of alphabetically organized high-frequency words that the children need to know how to spell. The process is simply that each child highlights the words as he/she uses the conventional spellings in his/her own writing. This has the positive effect of encouraging children to think about their spelling and to spell as many words as they can, as quickly as they can.

The format of such a record sheet is of little importance, but what is positive is the response of the child to being given the responsibility.

An individual *Words I Can Almost Spell* notebook is also a useful self-monitored spelling record, as well as a reference.

Date Begun: October 30

Name: Traci Hughes

Date Completed:

Aa	Bb	Ee	Ll	Oo	Rr
about	big	egg	like	of	ran
and	been	even	little	on	room
after	boy	ever	long	off	read
all	ball	every	look	one	road
are	before		left	our	run
at	best		let	out	
again	better		life	over	
am	book		live	once	
an		**Ff**	love		
around		from			**Ss**
asked		father			said
away		first			so
air	**Cc**	found		**Pp**	saw
along	came	family	**Mm**	people	she
also	call	fast	mom	play	some

Observing directional movement in letter formation during personal writing guides the focus for demonstrating specific letter formation in the context of shared writing.

HANDWRITING SURVEY

Observing directional movement in letter formation is an important assessment procedure that can be carried out by simply watching and noticing as a child is writing, and during analysis of writing samples.

This simple, easy-to-manage record* is a way of identifying individuals and small groups of children who need spe-

cific help in the directional formation of particular letters.

Demonstration of letter formation becomes a teaching focus during shared writing, individual writing conferences, and small-group guided writing sessions.

*Letter Formation Survey included as a blackline master at the end of this book. Also available as a separate record pad in Rigby's Evaluation Package.

SPEAKING AND LISTENING DEVELOPMENT

Most children will speak freely, inquire confidently, question naturally, report enthusiastically, and describe graphically when they know their language, thoughts, and feelings are respected and valued, and the context is relevant, meaningful, understandable, and enjoyable.

Our goals are to develop in children the ability to communicate effectively by means of speech, and to encourage in them the habit of listening interpretively, listening reflectively, and listening critically.

Effective planning for this growth is based on knowing and understanding the language usage, language preferences, cultural conventions for conversation, experiences and interests of individual children, and matching this with meaningful learning experiences that involve speaking and listening within a variety of curriculum contexts in the classroom.

Information is gathered and recorded over time as the teacher

• discovers the language(s) spoken at home

• observes individual children as they speak

• notices the situations/conditions where individual children are most confident to speak and most reluctant to speak

• notices the language a child prefers to use, and in what situations

• converses with and listens to children

• observes a child's willingness to initiate conversation, share ideas, and participate in small group discussions

• notices nonverbal behavior

• recognizes the need for specialized speech/hearing correction

Conversations can be recorded in anecdotal notes and matched against various speaking and listening continuum checks. Such checks should be collaboratively devised by teachers and should focus on monitoring the development of the attitudes, knowledge, and skills teachers are aiming for children to acquire in these modes of language.

These procedures help teachers to identify early any children who may need diagnostic analysis of speaking and listening development by a speech therapist and/or audiologist.

Records pertaining to speaking and listening development are added to each child's Cumulative Learning Profile. Specialist reports should transfer with the child to the next class/school.

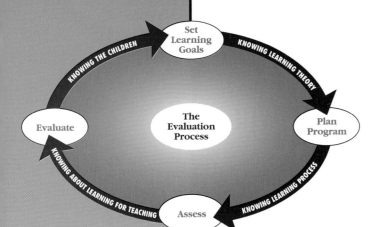

Set
Learning
Goals

KNOWING THE CHILDREN

KNOWING LEARNING THEORY

Evaluate

The
Evaluation
Process

Plan
Program

KNOWING ABOUT LEARNING FOR TEACHING

Assess

KNOWING LEARNING PROCESS

Children's
Self-Evaluation

7

ASSESSMENT PROCEDURES

Encourage children to

— share their views of themselves as learners, readers, and writers

— reflect upon what they have learned, and how they learned it

— set their own learning goals and challenges, and reflect upon their own success in reaching those goals

— talk about their choices and preferences in reading and writing

— identify personal challenges in learning, and how they cope with such challenges

— select samples of their own work, and articulate strengths and challenges

— talk with others about their reading, writing, and spelling

— reflect upon themselves and their relationships with others

RECORDS

children's personal selections of their own samples of work in various areas of the curriculum

those that are devised by the teacher for/with the children, or by the children themselves

t is frequently the children themselves who are able to provide the most illuminating insights into their own learning and social behaviors.

SELF-EVALUATION

When children come into our care, we enter into a partnership with them, and that means trust, respect, collaboration, and shared responsibility. As teachers, we should develop the habit of valuing children as experts in their own right.

It is the children themselves who best understand why they say what they say and do what they do. It therefore stands to reason that the learner, who is the

central and most active participant in the educational process, must also be central and active in the whole evaluation process.

If our goal is to develop independence in literate behavior we must ensure that we actually encourage self-evaluation of literate activity from the time that children first enter school. The demonstrations we provide of reflective questions to ask and positive ways to respond will act as a guide for children in talking with each other about their own learning.

Schedule times to share records from the cumulative learning profile with each child during the year. This is very positive and rewarding for the children, as they enjoy seeing how much they have learned over a period of time.

Self-evaluation by children will be encouraged and enhanced if we

- show children we value their own knowledge, experiences, and opinions

- develop the habit of giving feedback that is useful to the learner, e.g., "I noticed that you went back and checked what you had read; then you changed it. What made you do that?" instead of "Good boy/girl. That's right."

- develop the habit of "waiting and watching" when a child has made an error or is facing a reading, writing, or spelling challenge in a text. Encourage or prompt the child to give it a try, e.g., "What do you think it could be? Look at the illustrations. Can you find a clue there? You said ....Does that make sense? Can we say it that way? Say it slowly. What sounds can you hear? Look at the first letter in that word. Read it again and take a guess."

- are constantly alert to the fact that what we say to children when encouraging self-reflection and evaluation actually provides them with a demonstration of what we want them to say to themselves

- actively involve children in reflecting upon and recording their own development, progress, strengths, and needs in learning

Involving children in reflective analysis of their own knowledge, their learning processes, strengths, and needs develops the habit of objective self-evaluation.

Teachers and/or children themselves may devise forms for self-evaluation. The key to their value as an assessment tool is the way in which such forms respect and trust children as the experts in knowing how, what, and why they learn. Such forms should encourage objective self-analysis and develop the habit of reflective thinking about

- how they know what they know

- how they perceive their progress and needs in learning

- what they want/need to know next

- how they might go about finding out

- what they learned in the process

The following samples of self-evaluation forms show their value as an assessment tool.

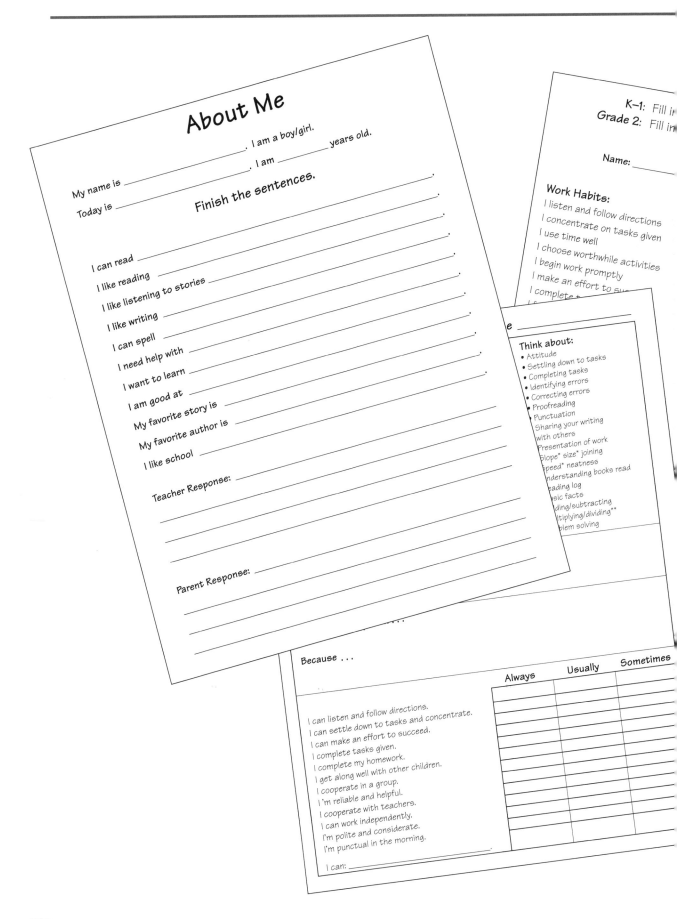

About Me

My name is _____. I am a boy/girl.

Today is _____. I am _____ years old.

Finish the sentences.

I can read _____

I like reading _____

I like listening to stories _____

I like writing _____

I can spell _____

I need help with _____

I want to learn _____

I am good at _____

My favorite story is _____

My favorite author is _____

I like school _____

Teacher Response: _____

_____

Parent Response: _____

_____

K–1: Fill i
Grade 2: Fill i

Name: _____

Work Habits:

I listen and follow directions
I concentrate on tasks given
I use time well
I choose worthwhile activities
I begin work promptly
I make an effort to su
I complete t

Think about:
- Attitude
- Settling down to tasks
- Completing tasks
- Identifying errors
- Correcting errors
- Proofreading
- Punctuation
- Sharing your writing with others
- Presentation of work
- Slope* size* joining
- Speed* neatness
- Understanding books read
- Reading log
- Basic facts
- Adding/subtracting
- Multiplying/dividing**
- Problem solving

Because . . .

	Always	Usually	Sometimes
I can listen and follow directions.			
I can settle down to tasks and concentrate.			
I can make an effort to succeed.			
I complete tasks given.			
I complete my homework.			
I get along well with other children.			
I cooperate in a group.			
I'm reliable and helpful.			
I cooperate with teachers.			
I can work independently.			
I'm polite and considerate.			
I'm punctual in the morning.			

I can: _____

or in discussion with a friend

Date: _____

	Always	Usually	Sometimes

Name:

Date:

I used to think . . .

Now I know . . .

Name:

Date:

I used to think . . .

Topic: _____

I think that . . .

I'll find out by:

I have found out that . . .

My Comments

The
Evaluation
Process

Set
Learning
Goals

KNOWING THE CHILDREN

KNOWING LEARNING THEORY

Evaluate

Plan
Program

KNOWING ABOUT LEARNING FOR TEACHING

Assess

KNOWING LEARNING PROCESS

The Cumulative Learning Profile CLP

8

ASSESSMENT PROCEDURES

all those discussed so far in this book

RECORDS

all those discussed so far

cumulative record

he ongoing records, together with the Cumulative Record,* which summarizes all of the information at the middle and end of each year, add up to present a cohesive, informative profile of a child's progress in literacy learning. It is a professional account of learning to share with the learner, parents/caregivers, colleagues, principals, and administrators.

THE CUMULATIVE RECORD

The Cumulative Record is a summary of the information gathered through ongoing assessment. It becomes a permanent statement of achievement and progress in learning, which transfers with a child to a receiving teacher or school.

It is intended to present an objective overview of a child's attitudes, interests, strengths, and instructional needs. This information provides the basis for comment in personal report cards, and the foundation on which contexts and programs for further learning and teaching are based.

*Cumulative Record is included as a blackline master at the end of this book. Also available as a separate record pad in Rigby's Evaluation Package.

Observing children in a range of contexts over time provides valuable information with which to build a CLP of each child's progress and achievement.

The information to be contained in this example of a summarized statement should include

1. first-week entry information
2. a six-week summary of observations
3. a six-month summary of progress and achievement
4. an end-of-year summary of progress and achievement
5. second- and third-year summaries of progress and achievement
6. a record of attendance

First-week entry

- On admission to school and/or during the first week, record

—name, school, date of birth, date entered first school

—health factors

—interests, strengths, and concerns

Six-week summary of observations

- At or throughout the first six weeks after entering school, check that for every child you have completed

—anecdotal records

—an alphabet knowledge check

—a running record

—an annotated sample of writing

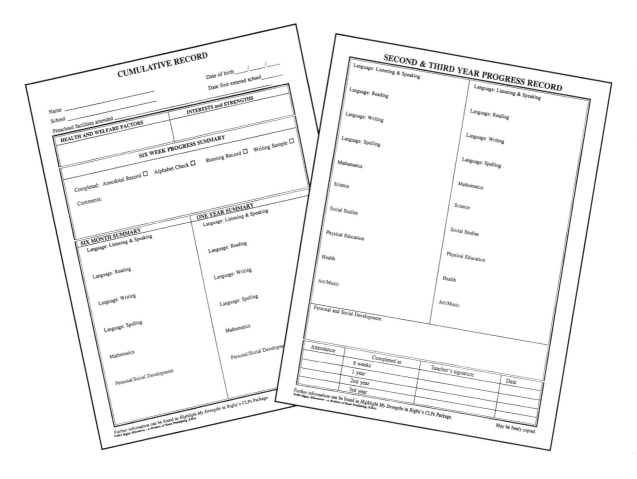

CUMULATIVE RECORD

Date of birth___/___/___

Date first entered school_____

Name _____
School _____
Preschool facilities attended _____

| HEALTH AND WELFARE FACTORS | INTERESTS and STRENGTHS |

SIX WEEK PROGRESS SUMMARY

Completed: Anecdotal Record ☐   Alphabet Check ☐   Running Record ☐   Writing Sample ☐

Comments:

SIX MONTH SUMMARY

Language: Listening & Speaking

Language: Reading

Language: Writing

Language: Spelling

Mathematics

Personal/Social Development

ONE YEAR SUMMARY

Language: Listening & Speaking

Language: Reading

Language: Writing

Language: Spelling

Mathematics

Personal/Social Development

Further information can be found in *Highlight My Strengths* in Rigby's CLPs Package.
©1995 Rigby Education – a division of Reed Publishing (USA)

SECOND & THIRD YEAR PROGRESS RECORD

Language: Listening & Speaking

Language: Reading

Language: Writing

Language: Spelling

Mathematics

Science

Social Studies

Physical Education

Health

Art/Music

Personal and Social Development

Language: Listening & Speaking

Language: Reading

Language: Writing

Language: Spelling

Mathematics

Science

Social Studies

Physical Education

Health

Art/Music

Attendance	Completed at	Teacher's signature	Date
	6 weeks		
	1 year		
	2nd year		
	3rd year		

Further information can be found in *Highlight My Strengths* in Rigby's CLPs Package.
©1995 Rigby Education – a division of Reed Publishing (USA)

May be freely copied.

- Write a summary of your general observations. Comment on such things as

  —adaptation from cultural context of home/previous class to cultural context of school/new class

  —social interaction within both the classroom and playground contexts

  —interests, strengths, learning preferences

  —instructional needs

  —attitudes, knowledge, and skills demonstrated in speaking, listening, reading, writing, and mathematics

  —aspects of learning, personal, and social behaviors that need closer observation

Six-month summary, end-of-year summary, and summaries thereafter

- From your ongoing records and general observations, write a narrative statement about a child's attitudes, interests, strengths, and needs in personal and social development, and his/her progress and achievement in all curriculum areas.

- Record any need for more intensive individual monitoring, instruction, acceleration, and/or early intervention.

- Record specifics of any individualized instruction for intervention and/or acceleration that have been applied.

ASSESSMENT PROCEDURES OVERVIEW

The assessment recording procedures shown in this portfolio are by no means a finite list, but they do present examples of those that are recommended most highly by teachers already involved in this holistic approach to assessment and evaluation.

The notion of developing cumulative learning profiles for a whole class of children—and managing and organizing a schedule for taking ongoing records—can present an awesome challenge, not only for the teachers who are just beginning, but also for those who are experienced.

There will always be the question of time: How can I possibly observe all of the children in my class and find the time to gather so many records? When do I fit it all in? How will I manage? What do I do with the others? There may be apprehension: How can I be sure that this approach will benefit my children?

Begin by looking closely at the following overview of the records. Consider the schedule and the information that stands to be gained. Decide upon your own comfortable starting point for including or adding some of these observational techniques into your classroom practice, and begin a CLP approach to assessment and evaluation of literacy learning.

In a classroom where children are encouraged to engage in meaningful, independent literate activity, the teacher is freed to observe and gather information in a variety of ways.

Ongoing Records	Schedule
Entry Survey	on entry to class or school
Anecdotal Records	entries on every child at least every 6 weeks
*Alphabet Knowledge Record**	at 6 weeks, 6 months, 1 year
Running Records of Text Reading	one with each child at least every 6 weeks (see page 30): not necessary to keep once information is transferred to summary sheet
*Running Record Summary**	6 weeks, 6 months, 1 year
Home Reading Record	as often as is manageable—entry made on day book goes home
*Reading Continuum Checks**	at least once every 6 weeks following each running record, more often if manageable
Cumulative Samples of Writing	at least one every 6 weeks
Self-Monitored Spelling Record	ongoing by the child
*Writing Continuum Check**	6 weeks, 6 months, 1 year, more often if manageable
Letter Formation Survey	informally any day as children write
Self-Evaluation Records	on a regular basis as children are ready to do this (likely to be less with 5-year-olds than with 7-year-olds)
*Cumulative Record**	entries made during week 1, and at 6 weeks, 6 months, 1 year, twice in each of second and third years maintained through years at school

*Transfers with child to receiving class/school.

Information

- background experiences
- health, family, interests

- patterns and themes of learning behavior
- insights into a child's view of him/herself as a learner

- progress in development of alphabet knowledge
- development of sound-symbol relationships

- attitudes, development of strategies for
  independent reading (see pages 25, 26, 27)

- brief, easy-to-see synthesis of most important information
  from ongoing running records

- family involvement
- child's attitude

- quick identification of general gaps in learning over a class
- matches observations to specific skills/strategies
- a quick reading behavior check

- development of writing and spelling

- progress in using conventional spellings of high-frequency words

- matches observations to specific skills and strategies
- overviews of strengths and gaps in writing development

- needs for specific help in directional formation of letters

- view of self
- attitudes
- interests

- a permanent summary of all information gathered before

Observing children at play also provides new insights into aspects of social relationships, personality, strengths, and interests that add to your developing profile of a child.

MANAGING CLPS

A way to manage this approach is to plan to watch one child (more if you feel that you can) very closely each day. Keep one question foremost in your mind: "What does this tell me the child knows?"

In the course of a day:

- Make anecdotal notes of your observations and conversations pertaining to social, reading, writing, and/or other relevant behavioral aspects.

- Take, analyze, and discuss a running record of text reading.

- Select, discuss, and annotate a sample of personal writing.

- Write a brief summary statement on a separate piece of paper and attach it to the above records. The statement should focus on a reflective comment about a child's attitudes, strengths, and ongoing instructional needs, along with your instructional intentions. These records are added to the child's CLP folder.

If you watch one child a day and complete the above records, you will manage to observe and record information on every child in your classroom at least once every six weeks throughout the year. As well, you will have time to schedule and record specific intervention and/or acceleration sessions with individuals or small groups of children within the context of the classroom program in action.

By six months and then certainly toward the end of the year, you will notice yourself becoming more confident, articulate, and assertive about your knowledge of any particular child in your class. You will find that through the process of observing and accumulating information, you "have the words" with which to make a sound professional statement of the progress, strengths, and instructional needs of every child in your class.

This in turn will help you to see clearly the implications for program planning, teaching approaches and strategies, resource selection, assessment and recording procedures, family involvement, and your own professional strengths and areas for professional development.

Getting started:

Getting started with CLPs in your classroom and/or school is both a personal and a collective collaborative process—a process of thinking and clarifying, talking, listening, reading, planning, organizing, managing, reflecting, and using trial and error.

For yourself personally, begin by thinking about and clarifying:

- your own vision of teaching and learning, what you value and are prepared to commit to

- your own philosophy of teaching, what you believe in, and what you care deeply about

- the role of assessment and evaluation in educational practice

- your own strengths and acceptance of who you are

- your knowledge of language learning processes

- your skills for observing learning behavior

- your own point for getting started

Developing school policy:

As a whole-school initiative, begin by establishing

- a collective school vision of teaching and learning, i.e., what you as a whole staff value and are prepared to commit to for the educational success of the children in your school community

- a consensus on philosophy of teaching and learning that is reflected in a "mission statement" for the school

- the particular strengths of individual teachers within the school, so that collectively these strengths form a solid foundation on which to base curriculum development, implementation, and systems for teachers supporting each other

- a cohesive policy for assessment and evaluation, so that observational and recording procedures are consistent throughout a school

- a cohesive policy for family inclusion, involvement, and reporting

As I said somewhere in the beginning, evaluation should be an integral, pervasive, and persuasive component of educational practice—its primary focus is to improve teaching and learning in our schools for today's children living in tomorrow's world.

Highlight My Strengths is a beginning, and the Rigby Evaluation Package a support, to help you on your way.

The processes, approaches, and techniques presented are philosophically and theoretically in rhythm with the most current information about literacy learning and teaching. They focus on highlighting the strengths of individual learners—on knowing and understanding how and what each child is learning, has learned, and needs to learn next. They are cognizant of individual differences and the developmental nature of learning. In this way they transcend the diverse philosophical, cultural, and physical differences in all classrooms and are appropriate, adaptable, and useful at all levels of the elementary school.

HIGHLIGHT MY STRENGTHS,
AND MY WEAKNESSES WILL DISAPPEAR.
Whaka paohotia ōku painga, kia ngaro ōku ngoikoretanga.

Blackline Masters

The following ten forms are provided as blackline masters. They are also available as separate record pads in the Rigby Cumulative Learning Profile (CLPs) Assessment and Evaluation Package.

Entry Survey

Entry Survey: "Getting to Know Me"

Anecdotal Record

Alphabet Knowledge Record

Continuum of Written Language Development

Running Record Summary

Home Reading Record

Letter Formation Survey

Cumulative Record (side 1)

Second & Third Year Progress Record (side 2)

Teacher/Family Conversation Record

ENTRY SURVEY

Name _____ Age _____ Date _____

Languages spoken:

Preferred language:

Type of preschool attended:

Health factors:

Special interests, strengths, needs, fears:

Parent expectations:

Teacher expectations:

Family members:

General observations of adaptation to school:

ENTRY SURVEY
"Getting to Know Me"

Name _____ Age _____ Date _____

My name

My age

My family

We live at

My friends

I like to

Reading is

Writing is

At school I like

ANECDOTAL RECORD

Name _____ Age _____ Date _____

Observations	Comments
Social:	
Reading:	
Writing:	
Health:	
Other:	

When to record? Try to record at least one observation in all of these areas every six weeks or at any time you notice significant shifts in behavior.

ALPHABET KNOWLEDGE RECORD

✔ = Correct response, i.e., Alphabet Name, Word, or Letter/Sound
◯ = Incorrect response
__ = No response

Name _____ Age _____ Date _____

Response to question "What are these?"   "You write with them."

G	T	M	L	Q	C	J
U	V	B	R	W	O	E
D	F	Z	S	H	X	N
K	A	Y	P	I		

g	t	m	l	q	c	j
u	v	b	r	w	o	e
d	f	z	s	h	x	n
k	a	y	p	i		

Total Correct _____   Preferred Mode of Response _____

Comments

©1993 Rigby Education - a division of Reed Publishing (USA)

CONTINUUM OF WRITTEN LANGUAGE DEVELOPMENT

Name _____ Age _____

	DATE OF ENTRY			COMMENTS
Pre-letter writing				
Writing letters, symbols or numerals randomly				
Left to right sweep of letters and some words established				
Random pointing when reading back				
Letter/word pointing when reading back				
Random use of high-frequency words				
Uses initial consonants				
Partial phonetic representation for word being spelled				
Left to right sequential arrangement of words				
Uses a few known words appropriately				
Complete phonetic representation for word being spelled				
Uses many words appropriately				
Reads back accurately at conference				
Spaces words appropriately				
Sequences ideas				
Rereads for sense				
Variety of topic choice				
Beginning to understand use of capital letters				
Beginning to hear and use medial vowels in words				
Beginning to hear and use end sounds appropriately				
Gaining control of directional movement in letter and word formation				
Writes own title				
Uses capitals correctly				
Uses periods correctly				
Marks approximations for discussion with teacher				
Developing control of systems for conventional spellings				
Maintains sequence of events over longer pieces of writing				
Uses a variety of styles - factual - imaginative - retelling - descriptive				

Further information can be found in *Highlight My Strengths* in Rigby's CLPs Package.

©1993 Rigby Education - a division of Reed Publishing (USA)

RUNNING RECORD SUMMARY

Name_____ Age_____ School Year_____

Title	Date	Level	S/US	% ACC	SC Rate	Comments

HOME READING RECORD

Name _____ Grade _____

Date	Title	✔ Read to child	✔ Read with child	✔ Read by child	Comments	Initials

LETTER FORMATION SURVEY

Name_____ Age_____ Date _____

Circle letters child needs help forming. Check each letter as formation is established.

a   b   c   d   e   f   g

h   i   j   k   l   m   n

o   p   q   r   s   t   u

v   w   x   y   z

A   B   C   D   E   F   G

H   I   J   K   L   M   N

O   P   Q   R   S   T   U

V   W   X   Y   Z

Further information can be found in *Highlight My Strengths* in Rigby's CLPs Package.

©1993 Rigby Education - a division of Reed Publishing (USA)

CUMULATIVE RECORD

Name _____   Date of birth_____/_____/_____

School _____   Date first entered school_____

Preschool facilities attended _____

HEALTH FACTORS	INTERESTS and STRENGTHS

SIX WEEK PROGRESS SUMMARY

Completed: Anecdotal Record ❑   Alphabet Check ❑   Running Record ❑   Writing Sample ❑

Comments:

SIX MONTH SUMMARY	ONE YEAR SUMMARY
Language: Listening & Speaking	Language: Listening & Speaking
Language: Reading	Language: Reading
Language: Writing	Language: Writing
Language: Spelling	Language: Spelling
Mathematics	Mathematics
Personal/Social Development	Personal/Social Development

SECOND & THIRD YEAR PROGRESS RECORD

Language: Listening & Speaking	Language: Listening & Speaking
Language: Reading	Language: Reading
Language: Writing	Language: Writing
Language: Spelling	Language: Spelling
Mathematics	Mathematics
Science	Science
Social Studies	Social Studies
Physical Education	Physical Education
Health	Health
Art/Music	Art/Music

Personal & Social Development

Attendance	Completed at	Teacher's signature	Date
	6 months		
	1 year		
	2nd year		
	3rd year		

Further information can be found in *Highlight My Strengths* in Rigby's CLPs Package.   May be freely copied.

©1993 Rigby Education - a division of Reed Publishing (USA)

TEACHER/FAMILY CONVERSATION RECORD

*Name*_____ *Age* _____ *Date* _____

| Discussion Points | |
Teacher	Parent/Caregiver
Personal & Social Behavior	
Areas of Strength	
Areas for Development	
Points Raised in Discussion	

Further information can be found in *Highlight My Strengths* in Rigby's CLPs Package.　　　　May be freely copied.

The following forms are provided as blackline masters and may be freely copied for classroom use.

Master Card of Alphabet Letters

Emergent Reading check

Early Reading check

Fluent Reading check

MASTER CARD OF ALPHABET LETTERS

G   T   M   L   Q   C   J

U   V   B   R   W   O   E

D   F   Z   S   H   X   N

K   A   Y   P   I

g   t   m   l   q   c   j

u   v   b   r   w   o   e

d   f   z   s   h   x   n

k   a   y   p   i

EMERGENT READING CHECK

Name _____   Age _____

	COMMENT	DATE
Enjoys listening to stories		
Chooses to read from various resources		
Can sit for a time and read a book		
Participates confidently in Shared Reading		
Retells stories and rhymes		
Likes to write		
Understands that writers use letter symbols to construct meaning		
Can show the front cover of a book		
Understands that the print carries the message		
Uses pictures as clues to the story line		
Knows where to start reading the text		
Knows which way to go, L—R, and to return		
Can point and match 1-1 as teacher reads		
Can indicate word		
Can indicate the space between the words		
Can recognize some high-frequency words both in and out of context		
Can write some high-frequency words independently		

Further information can be found in *Highlight My Strengths* in Rigby's CLPs Package.

©1993 Rigby Education - a division of Reed Publishing (USA)

EARLY READING CHECK

Name _____ Age _____

	COMMENT	DATE
Enjoys listening to stories		
Chooses to read independently		
Chooses to explore unfamiliar resources		
Beginning to take initiative for responding creatively to books		
Is confident to share feelings about books		
Participates confidently in Shared Reading		
Participates confidently in Shared Writing		
Developing ability to retell longer stories in sequence		
Developing ability to recall facts in informational books		
Writes with confidence and enthusiasm		
Developing ability to identify approximations in personal writing		
Takes responsibility for selecting words for personal spelling lists		
Less reliant on illustrations as a clue to make meaning		
Beginning to cross-check a number of meaning-making strategies when reading, e.g.		
• checks language predictions by looking at letters		
• rereads, or reruns to check		
• brings own knowledge of oral and written language to reading		
Beginning to check graphophonic detail as a means of confirming predictions		
Expects to get meaning from text		

Further information can be found in *Highlight My Strengths* in Rigby's CLPs Package.   May be freely copied.

©1993 Rigby Education - a division of Reed Publishing (USA)

FLUENT READING CHECK

Name _____   Age _____

	COMMENT	DATE
Enjoys listening to longer stories		
Enjoys listening to chapter-book stories as well as picture books		
Reads silently for leisure, pleasure and information		
Chooses to read independently from an increasing variety of genres for a variety of purposes		
Chooses to explore unfamiliar resources		
Reads chapter books and nonfiction informational texts of particular interest		
Expects to have independent control of first reading of an unseen text and demonstrates confidence when doing so		
Emergent and early reading strategies are secure and habituated		
Integrates and crosschecks language cues effectively		
Monitors and checks own reading with confidence		
Becomes more critical and reflective about the messages and information in text		
Expects challenges—demonstrates strategies for handling them		
Is able to summarize information		
Proofreads writing and shows increased knowledge of systems for conventional spellings		
Demonstrates a growing understanding of writing in different registers for different purposes		
Is able to locate information in index		
Contributes effectively in Shared Reading		
Contributes effectively in Shared Writing		
Confident independent reader, ready to go on reading to learn and using reading and writing as tools for learning		

Further information can be found in *Highlight My Strengths* in Rigby's CLPs Package.   May be freely copied.

BIBLIOGRAPHY

Anthony, Robert J. and Terry D. Johnson, Norma I. Mickelson, Alison Preece. *Evaluating Literacy: A Perspective for Change.* Portsmouth, NH: Heinemann Educational Books, Inc., 1991.

Cambourne, Brian. *The Whole Story: Natural Learning and the Acquisition of Literacy in the Classroom.* Auckland, New Zealand: Ashton Scholastic, 1988.

Clay, Marie M. *An Observation Survey of Early Literacy Achievement.* Portsmouth, NH: Heinemann Educational Books, Inc., 1993.

_____. *Becoming Literate: The Construction of Inner Control.* Portsmouth, NH: Heinemann Educational Books, Inc., 1991.

_____. *Observing Young Readers: Selected Papers.* Portsmouth, NH: Heinemann Educational Books, Inc., 1982.

_____. *Reading the Patterning of Complex Behavior.* Portsmouth, NH: Heinemann Educational Books, Inc., 1972.

_____. *What Did I Write?* Portsmouth, NH: Heinemann Educational Books, Inc., 1975.

Gentry, J. Richard. *Spel Is a Four-Letter Word.* Portsmouth, NH: Heinemann Educational Books, Inc., 1987.

Goodman, Kenneth S. and Yetta M. Goodman, Wendy J. Hood (Editors). *The Whole Language Evaluation Book.* Portsmouth, NH: Heinemann Educational Books, Inc., 1989.

Harp, Bill (Editor). *Assessment and Evaluation in Whole Language Programs.* Norwood, MA: Christopher-Gordon Publishers, Inc., 1991.

Heenam, John E. *Writing: Process and Product.* Auckland, New Zealand: Longman Paul.

Johnston, Peter H. *Constructive Evaluation of Literate Activity.* Longman Publishing Group, 1991.

Sharp, Quality Quinn. *Evaluation: Whole Language Checklists for Evaluating Your Children for Grades K-6.* Scholastic, Inc., 1989.

Tierney, Robert J. and Mark A. Carter, Laura E. Desai. *Portfolio Assessment in the Reading-Writing Classroom.* Norwood, MA: Christopher-Gordon Publishers, Inc., 1991.

INDEX

A

alphabet: 19-22, 25, 48

Alphabet Knowledge Record, The: 7, 8, 19-22, 61, 4; example 22; procedure 21-22

alphabet letters, master card of: 21

Anecdotal Record: 7, 8, 10, 15-18, 19, 23, 24, 64; example 18

anecdotal records: 42, 55, 61, 66; defined, 15; procedure 15-18

assessment: 57, 60; beliefs/purposes 5, 6, 7; defined, 3-4, 5; as key to child achieving educational potential 2, 10, 29; procedures (general) 6, 11, 20, 29, 63

B

bibliography: 86

blackline masters: 69-86

bookmarks: 39, 40

C

CLP: see cumulative learning profile

Clay, Marie: 23, 29, 30, 34, 35

conversations: with children 11, 16, 23, 43, 52, 55, 66; with family 12, 13, 14, 17; with educational colleagues 13, 17; among children 11, 15, 23, 43, 50, 55, 56

cumulative learning profile (CLP): 16, 43, 55, 56, 60-67; defined 6, 7, 60, 62

Cumulative Record, The: 7, 60-67

cumulative samples of writing: 7, 24

E

early stage: see *reading, stages of*

emergent stage: see *reading, stages of*

Entry Survey: 7, 8, 10, 61, 64; defined 13-14; example 14

evaluation: beliefs/purposes 5, 6, 7; defined 3-4, 5

evaluation process: 3-4, 56; diagram 4, 28

F

fluency stage: see *reading, stages of*

G

Gentry, Richard: 45

H

handwriting: 54

home reading: 25, 38-41

Home Reading Record: 7, 38-41, 64-65

L

learning goals: 4, 24, 25, 28, 32, 56

letter formation process: 43, 48, 54-55

Letter Formation Survey: 7, 8, 42, 64

O

observation: 3, 4, 5, 7, 8, 15, 45, 55, 61-62

Notes

Notes

Notes

Notes